French Grammar made easy

Rosi McNab

Hodder & Stoughton
A MEMBER OF THE HODDER HEADLINE GROUP

Orders: please contact Bookpoint Ltd, 39 Milton Park, Abingdon, Oxon OX14 4TD. Telephone: (44) 01235 400414, Fax: (44) 01235 400454. Lines are open from 9.00–6.00, Monday to Saturday, with a 24 hour message answering service. Email address: orders@bookpoint.co.uk

British Library Cataloguing in Publication Data
A catalogue record for this title is available from The British Library

ISBN 0 340 74926 1

First published 1999

Impression number	10	9	8	7	6	5	4	3	2	1
Year	2005	2004	2003	2002	2001	2000	1999			

Typeset by Wearset, Boldon, Tyne & Wear.
Printed in Great Britain for Hodder & Stoughton Educational, a division of Hodder Headline Plc, 338 Euston Road, London NW1 3BH by Redwood Books, Trowbridge, Wilts.

French Grammar Made Easy is a French grammar workbook aimed at adult non-linguists, that is adults with some rudimentary knowledge of French, who do not necessarily know anything about grammar, but need to learn about it so that they can progress beyond phrasebook French.

In the past, grammar has been seen as a barrier to language learning. It has put more people off learning a language than it has helped. Because of the way grammar has been portrayed, students were often made to feel that only those who could master 'conjugations' and 'declensions' could learn a language. In fact, you can drive a car without mastering the principles of the internal combustion engine – but if you do learn where to put the oil and how to check the tyres and fill up the windscreen wash, it does help!

Grammar is about recognising word patterns which give you a framework to a language; if you know the framework, you can 'build' new language of your own instead of having to learn everything by heart.

For those who already know some French grammar, short cuts are marked with 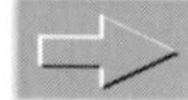 to enable you to go straight to the information you need.

A simple guide to the parts of speech

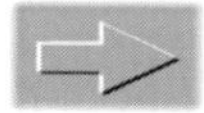

If you know what verbs, nouns, pronouns, adverbs, etc. are, go on to 1.1.

The most useful categories of words to recognise are:

1 Verbs – doing words

Verbs tell you what someone or something is doing.

I *am going* to France, My friend *booked* the flight, I *am going* to a meeting.

You also use them to ask questions . . .

Have you *seen* the film? *Are* you all right?

. . . and to give instructions.

Fetch it!, *Slow* down!, *Help* me!, *Wait!*

Verbs usually present most problems, so the section dealing with them is the longest one and comes first in the book.

2 Nouns – naming words

Nouns are the words which tell you:

- what something is;

  a *timetable*, a *train*, a *station*, a *town*, a *secret*
- who someone is.

  a *steward*, a *bank clerk*, a *baker*, a *student*

3 Pronouns

Pronouns are words which 'stand in' for a noun.

M. Bleriot is French. M. Bleriot lives in Paris.

Instead of repeating *M. Bleriot*, you can say *he*.

M. Bleriot is French. *He* lives in Paris.

In the same way, you can say *she* instead of repeating Florence in the following sentence.

Florence works in Strasbourg. *She* works at the European Parliament.

These are also pronouns: *I*, *you*, *it*, *one*, *we*, *they*, *me*, *us*, *them*.

4 Adjectives

Adjectives are describing words. They are used to describe something or someone.

the *new* house, the *red* car, a *tiny* flat, a *wet* day, a *busy* secretary

5 Adverbs

Adverbs are words which usually describe a verb, e.g. they describe how something is 'done'. They usually answer the question *How?* and in English, they often end in *-ly*.

He runs *fast*, She eats *slowly*, It comes *naturally*!

6 Prepositions

Prepositions are words which usually tell you where something is, e.g. *in*, *under*, *on*. Words such as *to*, *for*, *with*, and *without* are also prepositions.

1

Verbs

1.1 The infinitive

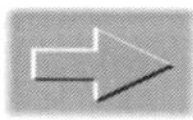

If you know what the infinitive is, go on to 1.2.

When you look up a verb in a dictionary, you will find the infinitive. This is the 'name' of the verb. In English, the infinitive consists of *to* + verb, e.g. *to read*, *to buy*, *to travel*.

I Here are some French infinitives. You probably know some of them already or can guess what they mean. See how many you can match up with their English counterparts.

Try to look for similarities between the French and the English. Some are obvious: for example, **organiser** *means to organise. Others are less obvious, such as* **laver** *meaning to wash (a lavatory was the place where people used to wash) and porter meaning to carry (a porter was someone who carried something, etc.).*

a.	parler	to wash
b.	habiter	to travel
c.	organiser	to arrive
d.	entrer	to verify/check
e.	voyager	to invite
f.	porter	to live
g.	vérifier	to speak
h.	inviter	to carry/wear
i.	laver	to organise
j.	arriver	to enter

These are usually referred to as ***-er** verbs* because they end in **-er**.

II Here are some more -er verbs. How many of them do you know already? They all have to do with food and eating.

a.	manger	to appreciate
b.	dîner	to taste/try
c.	déjeuner	to consume
d.	apprécier	to mix
e.	goûter	to dine
f.	souper	to lunch
g.	verser	to season (add salt and pepper, etc.)
h.	déguster	to eat
i.	consommer	to taste/sample
j.	assaisonner	to have supper
k.	mélanger	to pour

If you find it difficult to learn new words, try to find a 'hook' to hang them on: e.g. ***manger****, a manger where you put the food for an animal. And if you have travelled in France, you will almost certainly have seen signs at places selling wine, saying* ***Dégustation****, which means they are inviting you to taste their wines.*

More than 50% of English words derive from French words or have the same stem. If you don't know a verb, try saying the English word with a French accent – you have a 50% chance of being understood!

III What do you think the French for these verbs would be? Cover up the French and see if you can work it out.

a.	to decide	décider
b.	to prefer	préférer
c.	to separate	séparer
d.	to turn	tourner
e.	to return	retourner
f.	to develop	développer
g.	to insist	insister
h.	to change	changer
i.	to continue	continuer
j.	to accept	accepter

New words made into verbs are usually ***-er*** *verbs: e.g.* ***faxer*** *= to fax;* ***surfer*** *= to surf;* ***monopoliser*** *= to monopolise, etc.*

1.2 Groups of verbs

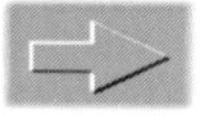

If you know how to find the 'stem' or 'root' of a verb, go on to 1.3.

In English, we just have regular and irregular verbs. A verb like *to dance* is regular . . .

dance, dances, danced, danced

. . . and a verb like *to fly* is irregular.

fly, flies, flew, flown

As you have probably already noticed, French verbs are more complicated! French schoolchildren have to spend years learning all about French verbs, but we can find some shortcuts. French also has regular and irregular verbs, but we usually divide French regular verbs into three main groups to make them easier to learn, depending on whether the infinitive ends in **-er**, **-ir** or **-re**.

group 1: *-er* verbs	**group 2: *-ir* verbs**	**group 3 *-re* verbs**
jouer regarder	finir dormir	répondre descendre

The stem, or root, of the verb is that part which is left after you take off the ending. It is used in making the other parts of the verb which you use to talk about the past and the future.

I Which group do these belong to and what is the stem of these verbs? (Remember: take off the -er, -ir, or -re to find the stem.)

a. vendre to sell (3/vend)
b. montrer to show . . . . . .
c. chanter to sing . . . . . .
d. sortir to go out . . . . . .
e. laver to wash . . . . . .
f. finir to finish/end . . . . . .
g. écouter to listen . . . . . .
h. fermer to close/shut . . . . . .
i. partir to leave . . . . . .
j. prendre to take . . . . . .
k. choisir to choose . . . . . .
l. porter to wear . . . . . .
m. rentrer to return . . . . . .

*Fortunately, over 80% of French verbs belong to group 1 (**-er** verbs) and they are mostly regular. When we say they are regular, we mean they follow the same pattern, so if you learn one, you can work out the endings you need for all the others.*

n.	venir	to come	. . . . . .
o.	dormir	to sleep	. . . . . .

1.3 Irregular verbs

Some verbs are awkward and don't really fit into any pattern. They are called *irregular* verbs. This means that you have to learn them separately, and, of course, they are the verbs you are likely to want to use most. Fortunately, you probably know quite a lot of them already, although you might not be aware of it: for example, you probably know that *I know* is **je sais** or *I don't know* is **je ne sais pas**.

These are the most important irregular verbs to learn, because they are the most used:

être – to be, avoir – to have, aller – to go

Most verbs which end in **-oir** and **-ire** are irregular, but they are also very useful.

***-oir* verbs**	***-ire* verbs**
devoir – to have to pouvoir – to be able to recevoir – to receive savoir – to know (something) voir – to see vouloir – to want	boire – to drink dire – to say écrire – to write lire – to read faire – to read rire – to laugh suivre – to follow

and all verbs made up of these verbs, for example:

écrire – to write → décrire – to describe
dire – to say → interdire – to forbid
rire – to laugh → sourire – to smile
faire – to do → refaire – to do again

Always look for patterns which will help you to remember new words, e.g. ***rire*** *– laugh →* ***sourire*** *– smile.*

I How do you say these in French? Complete the sentence by adding the correct infinitive.

	I would like to . . .	Je voudrais . . .
a.	eat	parler
b.	drink	acheter
c.	sleep	partir
d.	go	écrire
e.	talk	écouter

f.	do	boire
g.	understand	comprendre
h.	buy	suivre
i.	leave	aller
j.	finish	faire
k.	say	lire
l.	write	manger
m.	read	dire
n.	follow	finir
o.	listen	dormir

II Now read the phrases aloud. For example: a. Je voudrais manger.

You don't pronounce the ***-s*** *at the end of* ***voudrais*** *unless the next word begins with a vowel. If the next word does begin with a vowel, you run the two words together with a z sound.*

Je voudrais aller à Paris. *I would like to go to Paris.*

1.4 The present tense

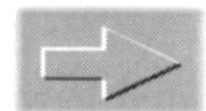

If you know about the 'persons' of the verb and when to use the present tense, go on to 1.5.

The present tense is used to say what you are doing now or what is happening now. In English, we have two ways of talking about the present.

We can either say what we are doing . . .

I *am reading*; My friends *are working*; It *is raining*.

. . . or we can say what usually/generally happens.

I *read* magazines; They *are* vegetarian; It *rains* every day.

In French, there is only one way of expressing the present tense.

Je lis le journal.	I read/I am reading the newspaper.
Ils travaillent à la Défense.	They work/They are working at la Défense.
Il pleut sur Paris.	It is raining/It rains in Paris.

In English, there is only one occasion when we change the verb ending: we add an **-s** when we are talking about someone else. This is called the 'he/she/it' form or the 'third person singular'. When we talk about ourselves, it is called the 'first person' and when we talk about you, it is called the 'second person'.

	singular	**plural**
first person	I talk	we talk
second person	you talk	you talk
third person	he/she/it talks	they talk

In French, the ending changes to show who is speaking.

	singular	**plural**
first person **second person** **third person**	je parle tu parles il/elle parle	nous parlons vous parlez ils/elles parlent

I	je
you	tu
he	il
she	elle
we (my friend and I)	nous
you	vous
they	ils
they (if they are all female)	elles

Tu is only used when talking to a child, a relation or very good friend. It implies a certain degree of intimacy and should not be used to address an adult unless he or she invites you to use it (see below page 22.)

There is no word for *it* as everything in French is either masculine or feminine, even a table and chair are feminine words.

Although **vous** is followed by a plural verb, it is the word you use for *you* in formal and professional conversation, even when addressing only one person. It is also used to address a stranger.

Ils is used for a mixed group of people (or things) if it includes one or more males, even if there are more females present. **Elles** is only used when everybody in the group is female.

Je, **tu**, **il**, **elle** etc. are called pronouns because they 'stand in' for, or represent, a person or thing. Mr Bloggs – *he*; Mr and Mrs Bloggs – *they*; Jim Bloggs and I – *we*, etc.

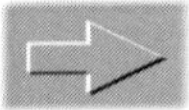

For more information on pronouns, go to 3.1.

I Which pronoun would you use?

a. You are talking about yourself: I am speaking.
b. You are talking about a girlfriend: she is always smartly dressed.
c. You are talking about a male friend: He has a weakness for fast cars.
d. You are talking about yourself and a friend: we are tired.
e. You are asking a child: Are you coming?
f. You are talking to a stranger: What are you doing?
g. You are talking about a group of women: they were discussing their boss.
h. You are talking about a mixed group or a group of men: they are attending a conference.

II And which pronoun would you use when you are talking about. . . ?:

a. your friend Paul;
b. your friend Martine;
c. Monsieur Leblanc;
d. Monsieur et Madame Lavoine;
e. Mesdames Leblanc et Bouvoir;
f. Sylvie et Charlotte;
g. yourself;
h. Paul, Guillaume et Martine;
i. Messieurs Meugeot, Briand et Duclos;
j. yourself and your friend.

1.5 Talking about yourself: *je*

1.5.1 Regular -er verbs

In the **je** form (or first person) of the present tense, all **-er** verbs end in **-e**, but the **-e** is not pronounced. Try reading them aloud.

*é (e acute or **accent aigu**) sounds 'ay', and **è** (e grave or **accent grave**) sounds 'eh'.*

infinitive	**meaning**	**first person**	**meaning**
aimer	to like	j'aime	I like
décider	to decide	je décide	I decide/I am deciding
écouter	to listen	j'écoute	I listen/I am listening
habiter	to live	j'habite	I live/I am living
jouer	to play	je joue	I play/I am playing
manger	to eat	je mange	I eat/I am eating
parler	to speak	je parle	I speak/I am speaking
porter	to wear	je porte	I wear/I am wearing
regarder	to watch	je regarde	I watch/I am watching
travailler	to work	je travaille	I work/I am working

I How would you say these in French?

a. I speak English. Je . . . . . . anglais.
b. I eat cheese. Je . . . . . . du fromage.
c. I am wearing jeans. Je . . . . . . un jean.
d. I work in an office. Je . . . . . . dans un bureau.
e. I am watching the news. Je . . . . . . les nouvelles.

f.	I play tennis.	Je . . . . . . au tennis.
g.	I like the town.	J'. . . . . . la ville.
h.	I am listening to a CD.	J'. . . . . . un compact.
i.	I live in England.	J'. . . . . . en Angleterre.
j.	I am deciding about the firm's policies.	Je . . . . . . de la politique de l'entreprise.

Now cover up the right-hand side of the page and see if you can do them again. Say them aloud!

II These are all -er verbs. Fill in the gaps:

a.	Je . . . . . . dans un bureau. (travailler)	I work in an office.
b.	J'. . . . . . à huit heures. (arriver)	I arrive at 8 o'clock.
c.	Je . . . . . . ma voiture. (garer)	I park my car.
d.	J'. . . . . . dans l'immeuble. (entrer)	I enter the building.
e.	Je . . . . . . le concierge. (saluer)	I greet the caretaker.
f.	Je . . . . . . au huitième étage. (monter)	I go up to the eighth floor.
g.	Je . . . . . . le code d'entrée. (composer)	I key in the door code.
h.	J'. . . . . . dans mon bureau. (entrer)	I go into my office.
i.	J'. . . . . . mon manteau derrière la porte. (accrocher)	I hang my coat up behind the door.
j.	Je . . . . . . à travailler. (commencer)	I begin to work.

Choose five of the verbs which you didn't know before (or had forgotten) and which you think would be useful for you to learn. Write down the meaning and the first letter of the verb. See how many you can remember.

1.5.2 -er verbs which change their spelling

Some **-er** verbs take an accent, change the accent or modify the spelling in the first person. This is because of changes in the way words are pronounced. They all still end in **-e**.

III Read the following verbs aloud. Remember that j **sounds like the** s **in treasure,** é **sounds like** ay **and** è **sounds like** eh.

a.	acheter – **to buy** → ash-e-tay	j'achète → jash-ett
b.	espérer – **to hope** → ay-spay-ray	j'espère → jes-pear
c.	lever – **to lift** → luv-vay	je lève → je lev
d.	préférer – **to prefer** → pray-fay-ray	je préfère → je pray-fair

Verbs with a **y** in them usually change the **y** to **i** (as in some English verbs: *dry* → *dries*).

e.	essayer – to try → es-say-ay	j'essaie → jes-say
f.	payer – to pay (for) → pay-ay	je paie → je pay
g.	envoyer – to send → ahn-v-why-ay	j'envoie → jahn-v-why

Some verbs double the **t** or **l**.

h.	appeler – to call → apple-ay	j'appelle → jappel
i.	jeter – to throw (away) → jut-ay	je jette → je jet

1.5.3 Irregular -er verbs

The most common irregular **-er** verb is **aller** (*to go*). Its first-person form is **je vais** (*I go/I am going*). The **s** is only pronounced if the next word begins with a vowel.

IV How would you say . . .?

a.	I am going to town.	Je . . . . . . en ville. (aller)
b.	I am buying a new car.	J'. . . . . . une nouvelle voiture. (acheter)
c.	I am calling my office.	J'. . . . . . mon bureau. (appeler)
d.	I prefer beer.	Je . . . . . . la bière. (préférer)
e.	I'm paying.	Je . . . . (payer)
f.	I am sending a letter.	J'. . . . . . une lettre. (envoyer)
g.	I hope it'll be fine.	J'. . . . . . qu'il va faire beau. (espérer)
h.	I am trying to answer the question.	J'. . . . . . de répondre à la question. (essayer)
i.	I am throwing out the rubbish.	Je . . . . . . les ordures. (jeter)
j.	I raise my glass to your good health.	Je . . . . . . mon verre à votre santé. (lever)

Highlight any verbs which you might want to use.

V Complete these sentences with the right form of the verb in brackets and read them aloud. Que faites-vous? **What do you do?**

a. Je . . . . . . anglais. (parler)
b. J'. . . . . . à Londres. (habiter)
c. Je . . . . . . à Paris. (aller)
d. J'. . . . . . à la gare. (arriver)
e. J'. . . . . . un taxi. (appeler)
f. J'. . . . . . dans l'hôtel. (entrer)
g. Je . . . . . . à ma chambre. (monter)
h. Je . . . . . . au restaurant. (dîner = to dine)
i. J'. . . . . . un fax. (envoyer)
j. Je . . . . . . une question. (poser = to put)
k. Je . . . . . . aux cartes. (jouer = to play)
l. Je . . . . . . cent Euros. (gagner = to win)

m. Je . . . . . . à mon ami. (téléphoner = to telephone)
n. Je . . . . . . la télévision. (regarder)

1.5.4 Regular -ir verbs

*Remember most verbs are **-er** verbs, so there aren't so many of these.*

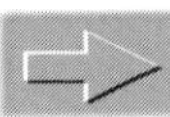

If you already know about regular -ir verbs, go on to the irregular verbs in 1.5.5.

infinitive	meaning	first person	meaning
choisir	to choose	je choisis	I choose/I am choosing
finir	to finish	je finis	I finish/I am finishing
grossir	to put on weight	je grossis	I am putting on weight
maigrir	to lose weight	je maigris	I am losing weight
remplir	to fill in	je remplis	I am filling in
vieillir	to grow old	je vieillis	I am growing old
applaudir	to applaud	j'applaudis	I applaud
réfléchir	to reflect	je réfléchis	I am reflecting
ralentir	to slow down	je ralentis	I am slowing down
rougir	to blush	je rougis	I am blushing

*Remember that in French you don't sound the final **-s** unless the next word begins with a vowel.*

VI Which verb would you use?

a. You have to fill in this form.
b. He has to finish the test.
c. She has to put on more weight.
d. He has to lose weight.
e. You have to choose a prize.
f. We have to think about it.
g. You must slow down at the bend.
h. You have to clap when they have finished.
i. You have to try to grow old gracefully.
j. Don't blush!

1.5.5 Semi-irregular and irregular -ir verbs

These verbs are sometimes called semi-irregular because they drop the final consonant of the stem and then add **-s**, which is not pronounced.

infinitive	meaning	first person	meaning
dormir	to sleep	je dors	I sleep/I am sleeping
partir	to leave	je pars	I leave/ I am leaving
sentir	to smell	je sens	I smell
sortir	to go out	je sors	I go out/I am going out

VII Practise saying them aloud, it will help you to remember them. The s is in brackets to remind you not to pronounce it!

je choisi(s)	je fini(s)	je grossi(s)	je maigri(s)
je pars(s)	je sen(s)	je sor(s)	je dor(s)

If you feel self-conscious about reading aloud, put your hands over your ears whilst you do it. This means that you don't need to speak so loudly and you can hear yourself better. If you haven't tried it before, try it now. It really works!

VIII How would you say the following?

a. I am going out. Je . . . . (sortir)
b. I am finishing the dishes. Je . . . . . . la vaiselle. (finir)
c. I am choosing a wine. Je . . . . . . un vin. (choisir)
d. I am leaving tomorrow. Je . . . . . . demain. (partir)
e. I am putting on weight. Je . . . . (grossir)
f. I sleep in a big bed. Je . . . . . . dans un grand lit. (dormir)
g. I slow down at the bends. Je . . . . . . dans les virages. (ralentir)
h. I am thinking about it. J'y . . . . (réfléchir)
i. I am filling in this form. Je . . . . . . ce formulaire. (remplir)
j. I am getting old! Je . . . . . . ! (vieillir)

Now cover up the right-hand side of the page and see if you can still do them.

The following verbs add an **i**, but they still end in **s** (which is not pronounced).

infinitive	meaning	first person	meaning
tenir	to hold	je tiens	I hold/I am holding
venir	to come	je viens	I come/I am coming

And there are some verbs which end in **-ir** which behave as though they end in **-er**.

infinitive	meaning	first person	meaning
ouvrir	to open	j'ouvre	I open/I am opening
couvrir	to cover	je couvre	I cover/I am covering
découvrir	to discover	je découvre	I discover/I am discovering
offrir	to offer	j'offre	I offer/I am offering

IX How would you say the following?

a.	I am coming from the office.	...... du bureau. (venir)
b.	I am offering some flowers.	...... des fleurs. (offrir)
c.	I discover the truth.	...... la vérité. (découvrir)
d.	I am holding the baby.	...... le bébé. (tenir)
e.	I am covering the baby.	...... le bébé. (couvrir)
f.	I am opening the window.	...... la fenêtre. (ouvrir)

Say them aloud to get used to the sound of the words. Which ones sound a little like the English?

1.5.6 Verbs which end in -oir

These verbs look as if they end in **-ir**, but they actually end in **-oir**, so they are a bit different. Unfortunately, they are verbs that you will probably need a lot, so you should learn them. Look for patterns to help you remember them.

infinitive	meaning	first person	meaning
avoir	to have	j'ai	I have
savoir	to know	je sais	I know
devoir	to have to	je dois	I must/I have to
voir	to see	je vois	I see
recevoir	to receive	je reçois	I receive/I am receiving
apercevoir	to notice	j'aperçois	I notice
pouvoir	to be able	je peux	I can/I am able
vouloir	to want	je veux	I want

X How would you say the following? Use the verbs in brackets.

a.	I have a brother.	...... un frère. (avoir)
b.	I have to go.	...... partir. (devoir)
c.	I know!	...... ! (savoir)
d.	I can come.	...... venir. (pouvoir)
e.	I must arrive punctually.	...... arriver à l'heure. (devoir)
f.	I want to go there.	...... y aller. (vouloir)
g.	I see the house.	...... la maison. (voir)
h.	I can speak Spanish.	...... parler espagnol. (savoir)
i.	I have a new car.	...... une nouvelle voiture. (avoir)

Cover up the French. Can you still do them?

1.5.7 -re verbs

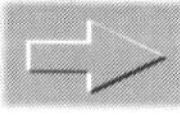

If you already know about regular -re verbs, go on to 1.5.8.

infinitive	meaning	first person	meaning
attendre	to wait (for)	j'attends	I wait/I am waiting (for)
descendre	to go down	je descends	I go down/I am going down
entendre	to hear	j'entends	I hear
répondre	to reply	je réponds	I reply/I am replying
vendre	to sell	je vends	I sell/I am selling

Cover up the meanings and see how many you know or can work out. Try to find a 'related' English word, e.g. ***vendre*** *→ vendor. Look for ways of remembering the ones that you think are important for you.*

These verbs all end in **-s** when you are talking about yourself (in the first person singular), but remember you do not pronounce the **-s** at the end of a word. Practise saying them aloud, as it will help you to remember them.

XI How would you say the following?

a.	I am selling my car.	...... ma voiture. (vendre)
b.	I am replying to the question.	...... à la question. (répondre)
c.	I am going down the road.	...... la rue. (descendre)
d.	I am waiting for the bus.	...... le bus. (attendre)
e.	I hear some voices.	...... des voix. (entendre)

Now cover up the right-hand side of the page and see if you can still do them.

1.5.8 Irregular -re verbs

These verbs end in **-re** but sometimes they change their stem. The changes have usually been made to make them easier to pronounce. These are the ones you are likely to need most. Say them aloud and look for patterns.

infinitive	meaning	first person	meaning
être	to be	je suis	I am
boire	to drink	je bois	I drink/I am drinking
croire	to believe	je crois	I believe
dire	to say	je dis	I say/I am saying

infinitive	meaning	first person	meaning
écrire	to write	j'écris	I write/I am writing
faire	to do/make	je fais	I do/I am doing
lire	to read	je lis	I read/I am reading
connaître	to know	je connais	I know (a person or thing)
mettre	to put	je mets	I put/I am putting
prendre	to take	je prends	I take/I am taking

Cover up the English and see if you can remember what they all mean, then cover up the French and see how many you can remember. Which ones sound really different from what you would expect?

XII How would you say the following? Remember that it is helpful to say the sentences aloud.

a. I am drinking red wine. ...... du vin rouge. (boire)
b. I am writing a letter. ...... une lettre. (écrire)
c. I do sport. ...... du sport. (faire)
d. I read the newspaper. ...... le journal. (lire)
e. I lay the table. ...... la table. (mettre)
f. I am English speaking. ...... anglophone. (être)
g. I am saying 'hello'. ...... «Bonjour». (dire)
h. I am describing M. Bonnard. ...... M. Bonnard. (décrire)
i. I believe in God. ...... en Dieu. (croire)
j. I am taking the train. ...... le train. (prendre)

1.5.9 How to say '*no*'

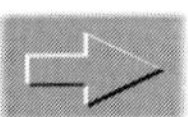

If you know how to use** ne . . . pas, **go on to 1.5.10.

To say you don't do something, you put **ne** in front of the verb and **pas** after it.

Je ne sais pas. I don't know.

Note that **ne** becomes **n'** before a vowel.

Je n'ai pas de . . .

XIII Say you don't do these things by putting ne **in front of the verb and** pas **after it. Say the sentences aloud to get used to the sound.**

a. I haven't a pen. Je ...... de stylo. (avoir)
b. I'm not French. Je ...... français(e). (être)
c. I'm not going to town. Je ...... en ville. (aller)
d. I don't drink wine. Je ...... de vin. (boire)

e.	I don't write letters.	Je . . . . . . de lettres. (écrire)
f.	I don't do sport.	Je . . . . . . de sport. (faire)
g.	I don't read magazines.	Je . . . . . . de revues. (lire)
h.	I don't know!	Je . . . . . . ! (savoir)
i.	I don't see.	Je . . . . (voir)
j.	I am not coming.	Je . . . . (venir)
k.	I can't go.	Je . . . . . . y aller. (pouvoir)
l.	I don't want to go there.	Je . . . . . . y aller. (vouloir)
m.	I don't eat snails.	Je . . . . . . d'escargots. (manger)
n.	I am not going out this evening.	Je . . . . . . ce soir. (sortir)
o	I don't watch TV.	Je . . . . . . la télévision. (regarder)

1.5.10 Reflexive verbs

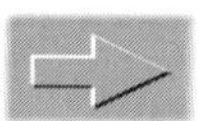

If you know about reflexive verbs, go on to 1.5.11.

We don't have an equivalent form in English but you probably already know the reflexive verb **s'appeler**, *to be called*. **Je m'appelle** means *I am called* or literally *I call myself*. The infinitive is **s'appeler**.

When you are talking about yourself, you use **me** (or **m'** if the verb begins with a vowel) and the first person of the verb, just as normal.

infinitive	meaning	first person	meaning
s'asseoir	to sit down	je m'assieds	I sit down/I am sitting down
s'endormir	to fall asleep	je m'endors	I fall asleep/I am falling asleep
s'ennuyer	to get bored	je m'ennuie	I get bored/I am getting bored
s'étonner	to be surprised	je m'étonne	I am surprised
s'habiller	to dress yourself/ to get dressed	je m'habille	I get dressed/I am getting dressed
se coucher	to go to bed	je me couche	I go to bed/I am going to bed
se doucher	to shower yourself/ to have a shower	je me douche	I have a shower/I am having a shower
se laver	to wash yourself/ to get washed	je me lave	I wash (myself)/I am washing (myself)
se lever	to get up	je me lève	I get up/I am getting up
se réveiller	to wake up	je me réveille	I wake up/I am waking up

XIV How would you say the following?

a. I wake up at seven o'clock. ...... à sept heures.
b. I get up straight away. ...... toute de suite.
c. I am washing my hair. ...... les cheveux.
d. I am having a shower.
e. I get dressed.
f. I sit down.
g. I am surprised.
h. I am getting bored.
j. I am going to bed.

1.5.11 Quickie

- When talking about yourself in the present tense, you use *je* and the right part of the verb.
- To find the right part of the verb, you take off the *-er/-ir/-re* ending.
- If it is an *-er* verb, you put the *-e* back, but you do not pronounce it.
- Most other verbs add an *-s*, but you do not pronounce the *s* either.
- The most important irregular verbs to remember are:
  avoir – to have → j'ai
  être – to be → je suis
  aller – to go → je vais
  faire – to do → je fais

1.6 Talking about yourself and someone else: *nous*

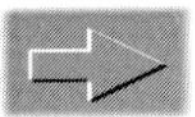

If you are not going to need to use this form, skip the rest of this section, and go to 1.6.5, as you need to be able to recognise it when you hear it, even if you don't use it.

You use the **nous** form (or the first person plural) where you use *we* in English, i.e. when talking about yourself and someone else: *we*, *my husband and I*, *my colleagues and I*, *my friend and I*, *Mrs Brown and I*, etc.

1.6.1 The *nous* form of regular verbs

The **nous** form is regular in most verbs. It is made by adding **-ons** to the stem. (Remember: the stem is made by taking the **-er**/**-ir**/**-re** off the infinitive.)

infinitive	first person pl.	meaning
arriver	nous arrivons	we arrive/we are arriving
aller	nous allons	we go/we are going
sortir	nous sortons	we leave/we are leaving
répondre	nous répondons	we answer/we are answering
parler	nous parlons	we talk/we are talking
jouer	nous jouons	we play/we are playing

I How would you say the following? Use the verb given at the end of the sentence.

a. We are working today. ......aujourd'hui. (travailler)
b. We are playing volleyball tonight. ...... au volley ce soir. (jouer)
c. We are leaving the house at 6 p.m. ...... de la maison à 18h00. (partir)
d. We are dining in a restaurant. ...... au restaurant. (dîner)
e. We are going back home at 10 p.m. ...... à 22h00. (rentrer)
f. We are going to Paris tomorrow. ...... à Paris demain. (aller)
g. We are leaving at 8 a.m. ...... à 8h00. (partir)
h. We arrive at 11.15 a.m. ...... à 11h15. (arriver)
i. We buy our tickets at the station. ...... nos billets à la gare. (acheter)
j. We have lots of luggage. ...... beaucoup de bagages. (avoir)

1.6.2 The *nous* form of irregular verbs

Some verbs change slightly in the **nous** form. Look for patterns to help you to remember them.

infinitive	meaning	first person pl.	meaning
faire	to do/to make	nous faisons	we do/we are doing
lire	to read	nous lisons	we read/we are reading
dire	to say	nous disons	we say/we are saying
écrire	to write	nous écrivons	we write/we are writing
boire	to drink	nous buvons	we drink/we are drinking
prendre	to take	nous prenons	we take/we are taking
comprendre	to understand	nous comprenons	we understand
avoir	to have	nous avons	we have/we are having
devoir	to have to	nous devons	we have to/we must
pouvoir	to be able to	nous pouvons	we are able to/we can
vouloir	to want to	nous voulons	we want to
voir	to see	nous voyons	we see
croire	to believe	nous croyons	we believe
être	to be	nous sommes	we are

Verbs ending in **-ger** (**manger**, **diriger**, **changer**, **nager**, etc.) add an **e** to keep the **g** soft, but are still pronounced as you would expect.

infinitive	meaning	first person pl.	meaning
manger	to eat	nous mangeons	we eat/we are eating
diriger	to direct/ manage	nous dirigeons	we direct/we are directing
changer	to change	nous changeons	we change/we are changing
nager	to swim	nous nageons	we swim/we are swimming

Some **-ir** verbs take **ss**.

infinitive	meaning	first person pl.	meaning
finir	to finish	nous finissons	we finish/we are finishing
choisir	to choose	nous choisissons	we choose/we are choosing

II How would you say the following?

a. We speak French. — Nous . . . . . . français.
b. We see. — Nous . . . .
c. We are choosing another day. — Nous . . . . . . un autre jour.
d. We are changing trains. — Nous . . . . . . de train.
e. We understand. — Nous . . . .
f. We are going to town. — Nous . . . . . . en ville.
g. We are eating in a restaurant. — Nous . . . . . . au restaurant.
h. We are taking the bus. — Nous . . . . . . le bus.
i. We are working late this evening. — Nous . . . . . . tard ce soir.
j. We are playing tennis later. — Nous . . . . . . au tennis plus tard.

1.6.3 *Nous* and the negative

This works in exactly the same way as the first person singular (**je**), i.e by putting **ne** (or **n'**) in front of the verb and **pas** after it.

III How would you say you don't do these things?

a. We don't speak French. — Nous . . . . . . français.
b. We haven't got a car. — Nous . . . . . . de voiture.
c. We aren't going to the cinema. — Nous . . . . . . au cinéma.
d. We aren't writing a letter. — Nous . . . . . . de lettre.
e. We haven't any milk. — Nous . . . . . . de lait.
f. We aren't reading *Le Monde*. — Nous . . . . . . *Le Monde*.
g. We don't watch television. — Nous . . . . . . la télévision.
h. We aren't coming tomorrow. — Nous . . . . . . demain.
i. We don't drink red wine. — Nous . . . . . . de vin rouge.
j. My friend and I haven't any work. — Mon ami et moi . . . . . . de travail.
k. We aren't tired. — Nous . . . . . . fatigués.
l. We aren't seeing Marc tomorrow. — Nous . . . . . . Marc demain.

1.6.4 *Nous* with reflexive verbs

The reflexive form is made by adding an extra **nous**.

Nous nous appelons Neil et Ruth. We are called Neil and Ruth.

infinitive	meaning	1st person pl.	meaning
se dépêcher	to hurry	nous nous dépêchons	we hurry up/we are hurrying up
se lever	to get up	nous nous levons	we get up/we are getting up
se coucher	to go to bed	nous nous couchons	we go to bed/we are going to bed
se promener	to go for a walk	nous nous promenons	we go for a walk/we are going for a walk
se reposer	to rest	nous nous reposons	we have a rest/we are having a rest
se séparer	to get separated	nous nous séparons	we get separated/we are getting separated

IV How would you say the following?

a. We wake up at seven o'clock. ...... à sept heures. (se réveiller)
b. We get up at eight o'clock. ...... à huit heures. (se lever)
c. We go to bed at 11 p.m. ...... à 23h000. (se coucher)
d. We are having a shower. (se doucher)
e. We are having a rest. (se reposer)
f. We are hurrying. (se dépêcher)
g. We are getting dressed. (s'habiller)
h. We are getting washed. (se laver)
i. We are going for a walk. (se promener)
j. We are getting separated. (se séparer)

Have you noticed that quite a lot of verbs which include 'get' in English are translated by reflexive verbs in French, e.g. get up, get washed, get dressed, get separated?

1.6.5 Quickie

- To talk about yourself and someone else (*we*), use *nous* in French.
- Most verbs have a regular first person plural, but there are some exceptions.
- Some verbs have minor spelling changes, but *être* is completely irregular (*nous sommes*).

V Match these English verbs with their French counterparts.

a.	we have	nous voulons
b.	we are	nous lisons
c.	we are staying	nous venons
d.	we are eating	nous ne comprenons pas
e.	we can	nous sommes
f.	we are not coming	nous pouvons
g.	we do not understand	nous arrivons
h.	we want	nous restons
i.	we are going	nous avons
j.	we are seeing	nous faisons
k.	we are leaving	nous ne venons pas
l.	we are arriving	nous allons
m.	we are coming	nous mangeons
n.	we are doing	nous partons
o.	we are reading	nous voyons

Now cover up the French and see if you can do them without help!

1.7 Talking to someone else: *tu*

This is the *you* form, or the 'second person' of the verb. There are two forms of *you* in French the **tu** form and the **vous** form. If you are talking to someone you know really well – a friend, a child or an animal – you use the **tu** form. You do not use it to a stranger, a business acquaintance or an older person. You use it to someone you know well, if they invite you to.

There is a special verb which means to call someone **tu** – **se tutoyer**. If someone asks: **On se tutoie?**, it means 'let's use the **tu** form' (**se vouvoyer** is *to use the* ***vous*** *form*).

The **tu** form is easy if you know the **je** form (see 1.5) as, in most verbs, it sounds exactly the same.

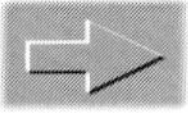

If you are not going to need the *tu* ***form, go to 1.8.***

1.7.1 Regular verbs

-er verbs

The **tu** form ends in **-es** but the **-s** is not pronounced, so it sounds just like the **je** form.

je mange → tu manges

-ir and -re verbs

The **tu** form is the same as the **je** form.

je finis, tu finis; je prends, tu prends

Exceptions

aller: je vais, tu vas
avoir: j'ai, tu as
être: je suis, tu es

I What is the tu **form of these verbs?**

a.	dance	**f.**	eat
b.	like	**g.**	listen
c.	live	**h.**	play
d.	speak	**i.**	wash
e.	watch	**j.**	work

II Use the right form of the verbs in brackets to tell someone what they are like.

a.	You are talkative.	Tu . . . . . . bavard(e). (être)
b.	You have got a spot on your nose.	Tu . . . . . . un bouton sur le nez. (avoir)
c.	You like swimming.	Tu . . . . . . la natation. (aimer)
d.	You eat pizzas.	Tu . . . . . . des pizzas. (manger)
e.	You watch soaps.	Tu . . . . . . les feuilletons. (regarder)
f.	You live in Paris.	Tu . . . . . . Paris. (habiter)
g.	You speak English.	Tu . . . . . . anglais. (parler)
h.	You wear jeans.	Tu . . . . . . un jean. (porter)
i.	You do sport.	Tu . . . . . . du sport. (faire)
j.	You play tennis.	Tu . . . . . . au tennis. (jouer)

1.7.2 Reflexive verbs

These are formed in the usual way. The reflexive pronoun is **te**.

III Match the questions. How would you ask a child . . .

a.	his or her name?	Tu t'intéresses aux animaux?
b.	at what time he/she gets up?	Comment tu t'appelles?
c.	when he/she goes to bed?	Tu ne t'intéresses pas à la musique?
d.	if he/she is interested in animals?	Tu te lèves à quelle heure?
e.	if he/she is not interested in music?	Tu te couches à quelle heure?

1.7.3 Asking questions

If you look at the sentences in 1.7.1 and 1.7.2 again, you can see that they can all be either statements or questions, both in English and in French. To make them into questions in French, you change the intonation by making the voice rise towards the end of the phrase.

Tu es fatigué(e)?	Are you tired?
Tu te reposes?	Are you having a rest?
Tu t'intéresses au football?	Are you interested in football?
Tu te souviens du jour où . . . ?	Do you remember the days when . . . ?

In French, you can also make a question by changing the order: invert the verb and pronoun. (This is one of those times when French is actually easier than English. In English, there are two different ways of forming a question, one for each of the two forms of the present tense.)

Habites-tu à Paris?	Do you live/Are you living in Paris?
Joues-tu au tennis?	Do you play/ Are you playing tennis?
Aimes-tu aller au cinéma?	Do you like going to the cinerma?
Ecoutes-tu les nouvelles?	Do you listen/Are you listening to the news?
Entends-tu bien?	Do/Can you hear well?
Manges-tu des pissenlits?	Do you eat/Are you eating dandelions?
Parles-tu bien l'allemand?	Do you speak German well?
Prends-tu le bus?	Do you take the bus?/Are you going by bus?

Practise saying questions to get used to the sound. Remember to make your voice rise towards the end. You will probably feel silly at first, but don't worry, practice eventually makes perfect!

IV Practise asking your friend what he/she is going to do. Just add the tu **form of the verb in brackets.**

a.	Have you got a meeting in London next Tuesday?	. . . . . . rendez-vous à Londres mardi prochain? (avoir)
b.	Are you leaving very early?	. . . . . . très tôt? (partir)
c.	Are you taking the Eurostar?	. . . . . . le Eurostar? (prendre)
d.	Do you get in to Waterloo?	. . . . . . à Waterloo? (arriver)
e.	Will you eat with us?	. . . . . . avec nous? (dîner)
f.	Are you going back the same evening?	. . . . . . ce soir même? (rentrer)

1.7.4 The negative

The negative is made in the usual way by putting **ne . . . pas** around the verb. Cover up the French and see if you can translate the English.

Tu ne parles pas l'anglais?	Don't you speak English?
Tu ne veux pas aller au Louvre?	Don't you want to go to the Louvre?
Tu ne manges pas de viande?	Don't you eat meat?
Tu ne m'écoutes pas!	You aren't listening to me!
Tu ne fumes pas?	Don't you smoke?
Tu n'as pas de regrets?	Aren't you sorry?

1.7.5 Quickie

- The *tu* form sounds the same as the *je* form.
- The *tu* form of *-er* verbs is the same as the *je* form, but with an *-s* on the end.
- The *tu* form of *-ir* and *-re* verbs is the same as the *je* form.
- Questions are formed by changing the intonation or inverting the verb and the pronoun.
- Negatives are formed by putting *ne . . . pas* around the verb.

V Chatting up – imagine you have already got to the tu **stage! Match the phrases, then cover the right-hand side of the page and see if you can remember the French translations.**

a.	Would you like a drink?	Tu veux une cigarette?
b.	Would you prefer a glass of wine?	Tu es fatigué(e)?
c.	Do you smoke?	Tu veux boire quelque chose?
d.	Do you mind if I smoke?	Ça te dérange si je fume?
e.	Do you want a cigarette?	Tu fumes?
f.	Are you hungry?	Tu préfères un verre de vin?
g.	Would you like to go to a restaurant?	Tu veux aller au restaurant?
h.	Are you tired?	Tu as quelqu'un dans ta vie?
i.	Do you like going to the cinema?	Tu aimes aller au cinéma?
j.	Have you got someone special?	As-tu faim?

1.8 Talking to someone else: *vous*

This is more important than the **tu** form as it is the form you will use most. It is sometimes also called the 'polite' form. Just like *you* in English, it can be used when addressing one person or more than one person, but it is always followed by the plural form of the verb.

1.8.1 Regular verbs

The **vous** form is usually made by adding **-ez** to the stem. It is easy to learn, and there are fewer exceptions than usual. It sounds like **ay** as in **parlez-vous?** You probably know a lot of words already.

Parlez-vous anglais?	Do you speak English?
Habitez-vous en France?	Do you live in France?
Avez-vous une voiture?	Have you got a car?

I What do these mean? Pair the sentences.

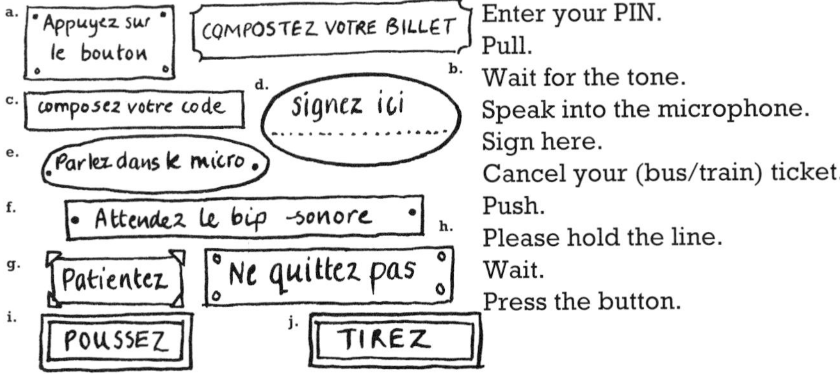

Enter your PIN.
Pull.
Wait for the tone.
Speak into the microphone.
Sign here.
Cancel your (bus/train) ticket.
Push.
Please hold the line.
Wait.
Press the button.

1.8.2 Irregular verbs

In most irregular verbs, the **vous** form is made from the same stem as the **nous** form. Look at these irregular verbs and try to find patterns which will help you to remember them. They are often like the infinitive, but not always!

aller	vais	vas	va	allons	**allez**	vont
avoir	ai	as	a	avons	**avez**	ont
boire	bois	bois	boit	buvons	**buvez**	boivent
connaître	connais	connais	connaît	connaissons	**connaissez**	connaissent
devoir	dois	dois	doit	devons	**devez**	doivent
dire	dis	dis	dit	disons	**dites**	disent
dormir	dors	dors	dort	dormons	**dormez**	dorment
être	suis	es	est	sommes	**êtes**	sont
faire	fais	fais	fait	faisons	**faites**	font
lire	lis	lis	lit	lisons	**lisez**	lisent
pouvoir	peux	peux	peut	pouvons	**pouvez**	peuvent
prendre	prends	prends	prend	prenons	**prenez**	prennent
savoir	sais	sais	sait	savons	**savez**	savent
voir	vois	vois	voit	voyons	**voyez**	voient
vouloir	veux	veux	veut	voulons	**voulez**	veulent

Comprendre is like **prendre**

II Tick the ones you know already. Highlight any which are different from what you would have expected and choose three new ones to learn.

III Your friend is not well. Give him/her some advice.

a.	You look ill.	...... l'air malade. (avoir)
b.	Go to see the doctor.	...... voir le médecin. (aller)
c.	Drink more water.	...... plus d'eau. (boire)
d.	Eat more fruit.	...... plus de fruits. (manger)
e.	Move yourself a little.	...... un peu. (bouger)
f.	Smoke less.	...... moins. (fumer)
g.	Go jogging.	...... du jogging. (faire)
h.	Get more fresh air.	...... à l'air frais. (aller)
i.	Go to bed earlier.	...... -vous plus tôt. (se coucher) (see 1.8.5)
j.	Sleep well.	...... bien. (dormir)

1.8.3 Asking questions

Questions are formed in the same way as the **tu** form: either by changing the intonation or by inverting the verb and pronoun.

IV Cover up the French and see if you can ask these questions.

a.	Are you going to the meeting?	Allez-vous à la réunion?
b.	Have you got an appointment?	Avez-vous un rendez-vous?
c.	Do you know the MD?	Connaissez-vous le P.D.G.?
d.	Do you know how to operate the video-link-up?	Savez-vous faire marcher le branchement vidéo?
e.	Can you contact your boss?	Pouvez-vous contacter votre chef?
f.	Do you have to go back to the hotel?	Devez-vous retourner à l'hôtel?
g.	Do you want to use the OHP?	Voulez-vous utiliser le rétroprojecteur?
h.	Can you see the screen?	Voyez-vous l'écran?
i.	Do you take notes?	Prenez-vous des notes?
j.	Are you making a recording?	Faites-vous un enregistrement?
k.	Are you ready?	Êtes-vous prêt?
l.	Do you understand?	Comprenez-vous?

1.8.4 Negation

As with other forms, you make a sentence negative by adding **ne . . . pas** around the verb.

V How would you tell someone not to do these things? First match the English and French, then cover up the right-hand side of the page and see if you can remember the French.

a.	Don't smoke.	Ne vous penchez pas au-dehors.
b.	Don't walk on the grass.	N'ouvrez pas la porte.
c.	Don't eat in the shop.	Ne mettez pas vos chaussures de ski sur le comptoir.
d.	Don't leave your luggage here.	Ne buvez pas cette eau.
e.	Don't cross the road.	Ne portez pas de noir.
f.	Don't lean out of the window.	Ne marchez pas sur l'herbe.
g.	Don't drink the water.	N'attendez pas ici.
h.	Don't wait here.	Ne mangez pas dans le magasin.
i.	Don't put ski boots on the counter.	Ne fumez pas.
j.	Don't wear black.	Ne laissez pas vos bagages ici.
k.	Don't open the door.	Ne traversez pas la rue.

1.8.5 Reflexive verbs

The reflexive pronoun for the **vous** form is **vous**.

Vous vous reposez?	Are you having a rest?
Vous vous débrouillez?	Can you manage?
Vous vous occupez de l'enfant?	Are you looking after the child?

VI Match the following English and French phrases, then cover up the right-hand side and see if you can remember the French.

a.	Can you manage?	Vous vous intéressez à l'enterprise?
b.	Are you interested in the firm?	Vous vous occupez des achats?
c.	Are you responsible for buying?	Vous vous débrouillez?

1.8.6 The imperative

The imperative is used for giving orders, instructions or directions. You use the **vous** form without the **vous**.

VII Let's try a keep fit session. Give the vous **form of the verb in brackets.**

a.	Come in!	...... (entrer)
b.	Get in a line.	...... les uns derrière les autres. (se mettre)
c.	Find a space.	...... une place. (trouver)
d.	Run on the spot.	...... sur place. (courir)
e.	Stand with your feet apart.	...... les pieds. (écarter)

f.	Stretch your arms.	...... les bras. (tendre)
g.	Pull your stomach in.	...... le ventre. (rentrer)
h.	Lower your shoulders.	...... les épaules! (baisser)
i.	Bend your knees.	...... les genoux. (plier)
j.	Put your hands on your knees.	...... les mains sur les genoux. (mettre)
k.	Don't move!	Ne ...... pas! (bouger)

VIII Tell some French visitors the way to the town hall.

a. ...... d'ici. (sortir)
b. ...... à droite. (tourner)
c. ...... la deuxième rue à gauche. (prendre)
d. ...... tout droit. (continuer)
e. ...... la place. (traverser)
f. ...... la rue jusqu'au rond-point. (suivre)
g. ...... à droite et la mairie est en face. (tourner)

1.8.7 Quickie

- The *vous* form of regular verbs is made by adding *-ez* to the stem.
- The *vous* form of most irregular verbs is made from the same stem as the *nous* form.
- Questions are formed by intonation or inversion.
- Negatives are formed by adding *ne . . . pas*.
- Reflexive verbs add the pronoun *vous*.
- The *vous* form is also used for giving orders and instructions.

1.9 Talking about someone else: *il/elle*

In French, everything is masculine or feminine. **Une maison** (*a house*) is feminine, so you say *'she' is old*; **un livre** (*a book*) is masculine, so you say *'he' is new*. Remember, there is no word for *it*, everything is *he* or *she*.

This form is called the 'third person'. It is easy to learn, as it sounds just the same as the **je** form. It is also used after **on** meaning *one*.

1.9.1 Regular verbs

- *-er* verbs end in *e* (just as in the first person, or *je* form).
  il/elle mange; parle; habite
- *-ir* verbs change the *-s* of the *je* form to *-t* (but sound the same).
  il/elle finit; choisit
- *-re* verbs don't usually have an ending, but they sound the same as the *je* form because the *-s* wasn't pronounced anyway!
  il/elle répond

I Find the right part of the verb:

a. Zinedine Zidane ...... au football. (jouer)
b. Céline Dion ...... des chansons en français et en anglais. (chanter)
c. Mon fils ...... sur l'Internet. (surfer)
d. Sa petite copine ...... les histoires de Stephen King. (aimer)
e. M. Berriot ...... des appartements. (louer)
f. M. Patte ...... sa maison. (vendre)
g. Mme Peugeot ...... une maison. (acheter)
h. La banque ...... l'argent. (prêter)
i. Le notaire ...... les documents. (préparer)
j. Mme Peugeot ...... devant le notaire. (signer)

1.9.2 Irregular verbs

The most common, and most useful, verbs are, or course, irregular!

infinitive	meaning	third person	meaning
avoir	to have	il/elle a	he/she has/is having
être	to be	il/elle est	he/she is
aller	to go	il/elle va	he/she goes/is going
faire	to do/make	il/elle fait	he/she does/is doing

II How would you say the following?

a. M. Patte ...... parisien. (être)
b. Il ...... à Paris. (habiter)
c. Il ...... à Nice. (aller)
d. Il ...... le train. (prendre)
e. Il ...... la nuit dans le train. (passer)
f. Le matin il ...... à Nice. (arriver)
g. Il ...... deux grandes valises. (avoir)
h. Il ...... ses valises sur un chariot. (laisser)
i. Il ...... signe à un taxi. (faire)
j. Quand il se ......, les valises ont disparues. (retourner)

1.9.3 Reflexive verbs

The reflexive pronoun for the **il/elle** form is **se**.

infinitive	meaning	third person	meaning
s'appeler	to be called	il/elle s'appelle	he/she is called
s'asseoir	to sit down	il/elle s'assied	he/she sits/is sitting down
se coucher	to go to bed	il/elle se couche	he/she goes/is going to bed
s'ennuyer	to get bored	il/elle s'ennuie	he/she gets/is getting bored
s'étonner	to be surprised	il/elle s'étonne	he/she is surprised
s'habiller	to get dressed	il/elle s'habille	he/she gets/is getting dressed
se laver	to get washed	il/elle se lave	he/she gets/is getting washed
se lever	to get up	il/elle se lève	he/she gets/is getting up
se réveiller	to wake up	il/elle se réveille	he/she wakes/is waking up

III Que fait Maurice?

a. Il .... (se réveiller)
b. Il .... (se lever)
c. Il ...... les dents. (se laver)
d. Il .... (se doucher)
e. Il ...... les cheveux. (se brosser)
f. Il .... (se raser)
g. Il .... (s'habiller)
h. Il .... (se chausser)
i. Il ...... son petit déjeuner. (prendre)
j. Il ...... de chez lui. (sortir)

1.9.4 Quickie

- The *il/elle* form of regular *-er* verbs is made by adding *-e* to the stem.
- The *il/elle* form of regular *-ir* verbs is made by adding *-it* to the stem.
- The *il/elle* form of regular *-re* verbs is the same as the stem.
- The most common irregular verbs are *aller* (*va*), *avoir* (*a*), *être* (*est*) and *faire* (*fait*).
- The reflexive pronoun for the *il/elle* form is *se*.

1.10 Talking about other people: *ils/elles*

This is easy, as most verbs sound just the same as for the **il/elle** forms in 1.9.

1.10.1 Regular -er verbs

The **ils/elles** form is the same as the **il/elle** form, but with-**nt** added (but not pronounced).

elle joue – **she is playing** → elles jouent – **they are playing**
il mange – **he is eating** → ils mangent – **they are eating**

However, if the verb begins with a vowel, you carry the **s** of **ils/elles** over to the beginning of the verb.

il aime → ils aiment (il-s-aime(nt))
elle adore → elles adorent (elle-s-ador(ent))

1.10.2 Regular and semi-irregular -ir verbs

The **ils/elles** form is made by adding **-ent** to the stem, but the **-ent** is not pronounced.

il court – **he is running** → ils courent – **they are running**
il dor(t) – **he is asleep** → ils dorm(ent) – **they are asleep**
elle peu(t) – **she can** → elles peuv(ent) – **they can**
*elle sor(t) – **she is going out** → elles sort(ent) – **they are going out**
*elle par(t) – **she is leaving** → elles part(ent) – **they are leaving**

*The **t** will now be pronounced as it is no longer the last letter of the word.

Some verbs take **ss**.

il finit – **he is finishing** → ils finissent – **they are finishing**
il choisit – **he is choosing** → ils choisissent – **they are choosing**

1.10.3 Regular -re verbs

If the stem has not changed, the two third-person forms will sound similar.

il attend – **he is waiting** → ils attendent (il-s-attend(ent)) – **they are waiting**
elle répond – **she answers** → elles répondent – **they answer**
il vend – **he is selling** → ils vendent – **they are selling**

*Remember, you only use **elles** if ALL the people (or things) are feminine. If there is one male in a group, however big the number of females, you still have to use **ils**. See 3.1 for more details.*

1.10.4 Important irregular verbs

These are verbs to watch because they change unexpectedly.

infinitive	third person singular	third person plural	meaning
aller	il/elle va	ils/elles vont	they go
avoir	il/elle a	ils/elles ont	they have
faire	il/elle fait	ils/elles font	they make/do
être	il/elle est	ils/elles sont	they are

1.10.5 More irregular (and useful!) verbs

Remember that you don't pronounce the **t** or **nt** at the end of a word!

infinitive	third person singular	third person plural	meaning
boire	il/elle boit	ils/elles boivent	they drink
dire	il/elle dit	ils/elles disent	they say
lire	il/elle lit	ils/elles lisent	they read
vouloir	il/elle veut	ils/elles veulent	they want
voir	il/elle voit	ils/elles voient	they see
pouvoir	il/elle peut	ils/elles peuvent	they can
devoir	il/elle doit	ils/elles doivent	they have to

I Qu'est-ce qu'il se passe? **(What happens?)**

a. M. et Mme Périgord . . . . . . faire des courses. (devoir)
b. Ils . . . . . . une nouvelle voiture. (avoir)
c. Ils . . . . . . à l'hypermarché. (aller)
d. Ils . . . . . . la voiture sur le parking. (garer)
e. Ils . . . . . . leurs courses. (faire)
f. Ils . . . . . . de l'hypermarché. (sortir)
g. Ils ne . . . . . . plus leur voiture. (trouver)
h. Ils . . . . . . partout. (chercher)
i. Ils ne la . . . . . . pas. (trouver)
j. Ils . . . . . . la police. (appeler)

II Typique ou pas?

What don't M. et Mme Meugot do?

a. M. and Mme Meugot don't speak English. — M. et Mme Meugot . . . . . . anglais. (parler)
b. They don't eat frog's legs. — Ils . . . . . . de cuisses de grenouille. (manger)
c. They don't wear striped jumpers. — Ils . . . . . . de pull à rayures. (porter)

d.	They don't drink red wine.	Ils . . . . . . de vin rouge. (boire)
e.	They don't spend their holidays at St Tropez.	Ils . . . . . . les vacances à St Tropez. (passer)
f.	They haven't got a car.	Ils . . . . . . de voiture. (avoir)
g.	They don't go to the cinema.	Ils . . . . . . au cinéma. (aller)
h.	They don't read *Le Monde*.	Ils . . . . . . *Le Monde*. (lire)
i.	They don't watch television.	Ils . . . . . . la télévision. (regarder)
j.	They don't live in Paris.	Ils . . . . . . à Paris. (habiter)

1.10.6 Asking questions: the interrogative

Remember, there are three ways of asking a question:

1. You can make a statement and change the intonation.
2. You can 'invert' the subject and the verb.
3. You can use a question word, and then invert the subject and the verb.

III Use method 2 to turn these statements into questions:

M. et Mme Leblanc habitent en banlieue parisienne.

a. Ils partent en vacances. → Partent-ils en vacances?
b. Ils prennent le train.
c. Ils vont sur la côte d'Azur.
d. Ils ont une maison secondaire.
e. Ils louent une voiture.
f. Ils jouent au golf.
g. Ils font du ski nautique.
h. Ils ont des amis, qui habitent à St Tropez.

IV Use method 3 with these question words:

a.	Where are they going?	Où . . . . . . ? (aller) → Où vont-ils?
b.	When are they leaving?	Quand? (partir)
c.	How are they travelling?	Comment . . . . . . à Paris? (voyager)
d.	Why are they in Paris?	Pourquoi . . . . . . à Paris? (être)
e.	What are they doing?	Que . . . . . . ? (faire)
f.	Who are they inviting?	Qui . . . . . . ? (inviter)
g.	How long are they staying at the hotel?	Combien de temps . . . . . . à l'hôtel? (rester)

1.10.7 Reflexive verbs

The reflexive pronoun for the **ils/elles** form is **se** (the same as the **il/elle** form). You will find that the singular (**il/elle** form) and the plural (**ils/elles** form) sound the same, as most reflexive verbs are **-er** verbs. Remember to pronounce the **s** if the next word begins with a vowel.

V Fill in the missing plurals.

infinitive	**meaning**	**third person singular**	**third person plural**
s'appeler	to be called	il/elle s'appelle	ils/elles s'appellent
s'asseoir	to sit down	il/elle s'assied	ils/elles s'asseyent
s'en aller	to go away	il/elle s'en va	ils/elles s'en vont
se coucher	to go to bed	il/elle se couche	a. ......
se doucher	to have a shower	il/elle se douche	b. ......
s'ennuyer	to get bored	il/elle s'ennuie	ils/elles s'ennuyent
s'étonner	to be surprised	il/elle s'étonne	c. ......
s'habiller	to get dressed	il/elle s'habille	d. ......
s'intéresser à	to be interested in	il/elle s'intéresse à	e. ......
se laver	to get washed	il/elle se lave	f. ......
se lever	to get up	il/elle se lève	g. ......
se réveiller	to wake up	il/elle se réveille	h. ......

VI Que font les amies de Florence et Véronique avant de sortir?

a Elles .... (se reposer)
b. Elles .... (se réveiller)
c. Elles .... (se lever)
d. Elles .... (se doucher)
e. Elles .... (se préparer)
f. Elles .... (sortir)
g. Elles ...... au bar. (aller)
h. Leurs copains n'...... pas. (arriver)
i. Elles .... (s'ennuyer)
j. Elles .... (s'en aller)

1.10.8 Quickie

- The *ils/elles* form of regular *-er*, *-ir* and *-re* verbs is made by adding *-ent* to the stem, and they mostly sound the same as the *il/elle* form.
- Some *-ir* verbs add *-issent (finir–ils finissent)*.
- The four main irregular verbs are *aller* (*vont*), *avoir* (*ont*), *être* (*sont*) and *faire* (*font*).
- Verbs ending in *-ire* or *-oir* are often irregular and need to be learned.
- The reflexive pronoun for the *ils/elles* form is *se*.

1.11 Short cuts

French verbs change the spelling of their endings according to the person who is doing them. Fortunately, most of them still sound the same except for the *we* (or **nous**) form, which ends in **-ons**, and the *you* (or **vous**) form, which ends in **-ez**.

Unfortunately, some of the most common verbs are irregular, but you probably know a lot of them already: **je suis**, **j'ai**, **je sais**, etc.

1.11.1 -er verbs

- Most French verbs are *-er* verbs.
- The regular endings for *-er* verbs are *-e*; *-es*; *-e*; *-ons*; *-ez*; *-ent*.
- All new verbs are *-er* verbs, e.g. *faxer*, *surfer*.
- Most *-er* verbs are regular, i.e. they follow the same pattern.
- Most endings sound the same, but the two marked * sound different.

habiter	
J'habite tu habites il/elle habite	Nous habitons* vous habitez* ils/elles habitent

1.11.2 -ir verbs

- There are not many *-ir* verbs.
- *-ir* verbs split into two different sorts: those which take *ss* in the plural (such as *finir* and *choisir*) and those which don't (such as *sortir* and *partir*).
- In the singular, the endings are *-s*, *-s*, *-t*, but you don't pronounce any of them, so they all sound the same.

finir	choisir	sortir	partir
je finis tu finis il/elle finit nous finissons vous finissez ils/elles finissent	je choisis tu choisis il/elle choisit nous choisissons vous choisissez ils/elles choisissent	je sors tu sors il/elle sort nous sortons vous sortez ils/elles sortent	je pars tu pars il/elle part nous partons vous partez ils/elles partent

1.11.3 Irregular -ir verbs

venir (*to come*) and **tenir** (*to hold*) are irregular, as are verbs made up of them, e.g. **revenir**, **retenir**.

venir	tenir
je viens tu viens il/elle vient nous venons vous venez ils/elles viennent	je tiens tu tiens il/elle tient nous tenons vous tenez ils/elles tiennent

1.11.4 -oir verbs

These verbs are not classed as **-ir** verbs, because they have a pattern of their own; they are, however, very useful verbs. Cover them up and see if you can remember their pattern.

devoir	savoir	voir	pouvoir	vouloir
je dois tu dois il/elle doit nous devons voud devez ils/elles doivent	je sais tu sais il/elles sait nous savons vous savez ils/elles savent	je vois tu vois il/elle voit nous voyons vous voyez ils/elles voient	je peux tu peux il/elle peut nous pouvons vous pouvez ils/elles peuvent	je veux tu veux il/elle veut nous voulons vous voulez ils/elles veulent

1.11.5 -re verbs

There are not so many **-re** verbs and most of them end with **-dre** and follow the same pattern. Most parts of the verb sound the same (those which don't are marked *).

répondre	descendre
je réponds tu réponds il/elle répond nous répondons* vous répondez* ils/elles répondent	je descends tu descends il/elle descend nous descendons* vous descendez* ils/elles descendent

*You do not pronounce **s**, **t** or **d** if they come at the end of a word.*

1.11.6 Irregular verbs

The following verbs are irregular, but you need to know them as they are used a lot.

avoir	être	aller	faire
j'ai tu as il/elle a nous avons vous avez ils/elles ont	je suis tu es il/elle est nous sommes vous êtes ils/elles sont	je vais tu vas il/elle va nous allons vous allez ils/elles vont	je fais tu fais il/elle fait nous faisons vous faites ils/elles font

Put a ring round the parts of each verb that you know already. Then try to find a way to learn the other parts. Look for patterns!

Remember that when you say I am going, etc., you do not translate the 'am'; you translate I 'go'.

I You are talking about yourself. Use the verbs in brackets.

a. J'...... un rendez-vous en ville. (avoir)
b. Je ...... prêt(e). (être)
c. Je ...... de l'appartement. (partir)
d. Je ...... le métro. (prendre)
e. J'...... à l'Opéra. (arriver)
f. Je ...... du métro sur la place de l'Opéra. (sortir)
g. J'...... Pierre et Bénédicte. (attendre)
h. Je n'...... pas attendre. (aimer)
i. Je .... (s'ennuyer)
j. Je ...... (rentrer)

II Now you are talking about yourself and a partner: Say we do (or don't do) the same things. For example:

a. Nous *avons* un rendez-vous en ville.

III Still using the same sentences, ask someone else if they do the same things. Use the vous **form. For example:**

a. *Avez-vous* un rendez-vous?

IV Now report back in the singular, saying he/she does it. For example:
a. Il/Elle a un rendez-vous en ville.

V Finally, say it in the plural: they do it. For example:
a. Ils/Elles ont un rendez-vous en ville.

1.12 The past tenses

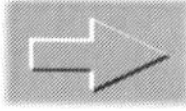

If you know when to use the perfect and imperfect tenses go on to 1.13.

1.12.1 The perfect tense (see 1.13)

In French, just as in English, there are lots of different ways of expressing the past tense. The one you will probably need to use most is the *perfect tense*, or **passé composé**.

I have eaten	j'ai mangé
I have arrived	je suis arrivé(e)

The perfect tense translates: *I played*, *I have played* and *I did play*, and the question forms *Have you played?* and *Did you play?* If you are talking or asking about something in the past, you usually use the perfect tense.

1.12.2 The imperfect tense (see 1.14)

This translates *I was playing when . . .*, *Were you playing when . . . ?* and *I used to play (a long time ago)*.

You use the imperfect tense:

- to talk about what used to happen in general;
  I used to go to school by bus. — J'allais à l'école en bus.
- to describe things in the past;
  It was always raining. — Il pleuvait tout le temps.
- to say what was happening when something else happened (an interrupted action).
  I was having a shower when he arrived. — Je me douchais quand il est arrivé.

1.13 The perfect tense

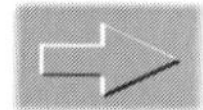

If you know how to form the perfect tense with** avoir **and** être **go to 1.13.1.

The perfect tense in French is made up of two parts like the English perfect tense: part of the verb **avoir** (*to have*) or **être** (*to be*) and the past participle.

to have	past participle	avoir	participe passé
I have he has we have	played spoken moved (house)	j'ai il a nous avons	joué parlé déménagé

Most verbs go with **avoir**, but some go with **être** e.g. **arriver**. Instead of saying *I have arrived*, in French you say *I am arrived*. To get used to the sound of the perfect tense choose one of the phrases, or make up one of your own and practise saying it until you are really fluent.

Je suis allé(e) au marché et j'ai acheté des tomates. — I went to the market and I bought some tomatoes.

Je suis allé(e) à la piscine et j'ai nagé pendant une heure. — I went to the swimming baths and I swam for an hour.

Je suis allé(e) en ville et j'ai fait des courses. — I went to town and I did some shopping.

Je suis allé(e) à la gare et j'ai pris le train de 18h00. — I went to the station and I got the 6 o'clock train.

Reminder

avoir – **to have**	être – **to be**
j'ai tu as il/elle a nous avons vous avez ils/elles ont	je suis tu es il/elle est nous sommes vous êtes ils/elles sont

Most verbs go with ***avoir***.

1.13.1 Verbs with *être*

The following verbs go with **être**. They are the 'going and coming' verbs, and fall naturally into six pairs. It is a good idea to learn them. Try making up a story, rhyme or picture using them.

aller – to go | venir – to come
arriver – to arrive | partir – to leave
entrer – to come in | sortir – to go out
monter – to climb/go up | descendre – to descend/go down
tomber – to fall | rester – to stay
naître – to be born | mourir – to die

All verbs made up of them, e.g. **rentrer**, **redescendre**, etc. also form the perfect tense with **être**.

I Who watched the 9 o'clock news? Complete these sentences by adding the right form of avoir.

a. Nous . . . . . . regardé le téléjournal de 21h.
b. J'. . . . . . regardé le téléjournal de 21h.
c. Il . . . . . . regardé le téléjournal de 21h.
d. . . . . . .-tu regardé le téléjournal de 21h?
e. Ils . . . . . . regardé le téléjournal de 21h.
f. Elle . . . . . . regardé le téléjournal de 21h.
g. Elles n'. . . . . . pas regardé le téléjournal de 21h.
h. . . . . . .-vous regardé le téléjournal de 21h?
i. Julie . . . . . . regardé le téléjournal de 21h.
j. Mes parents n'. . . . . . pas regardé le téléjournal de 21h.

II Who went to town? Complete these sentences by adding the right form of être.

a. Je . . . . . . allé(e) en ville.
b. Mon mari . . . . . . resté à la maison.
c. Mes enfants . . . . . . allés au Parc des Sciences et de l'Industrie de la Villette.
d. Ma mère . . . . . . restée à la maison.
e. . . . . . .-tu allé(e) en ville?
f. M. Hibbert . . . . . . allé au cinéma.
g. Sa femme . . . . . . restée à la maison.
h. Leur fils . . . . . . allé à un match de rugby.
i. . . . . . .-vous restés à la maison?
j. Nous . . . . . . allés au tiercé à Longchamp.

1.13.2 Agreement of past participles

You may have noticed that after verbs which go with **être**, the past participle 'agrees' with the subject. That is, if the person doing the action is feminine, you add an **-e**, if there is more than one person doing the action, you add an **-s**, and if there is more than one person and they are all feminine, you add **-es**.

None of these endings are pronounced so they are only important if you are going to write in French. See 1.13.6.

1.13.3 How to form the past participle of regular verbs

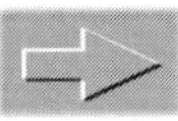

If you know how to form the past participle, go to 1.13.4.

In English, the past participle of regular verbs is formed by adding **-ed** to the infinitive.

play → played; watch → watched; dance → danced

In French, **-er**, **-ir** and **-re** verbs form their past participles in different ways. You take off the ending (**-er**, **-ir** or **-re**) and add the following.

-er **verbs**	-ir **verbs**	-re **verbs**
-é	-i	-u

parler → parlé; dormir → dormi; répondre → répondu

III Using these rules, what would the past participles of these verbs be?

a. jouer
b. manger
c. finir
d. vendre
e. écouter
f. perdre
g. choisir
h. attendre
i. organiser
j. inviter
k. laver
l. demander
m. fermer
n. pousser
o. tirer
p. oublier
q. sortir
r. entrer
s. entendre
t. partir

IV Qu'est-ce qu'ils ont fait hier soir? **What did Marc do last night? Add the right form of the past participle of the verb in brackets.**

a.	Après le travail, j'ai ...... au squash avec Jacques. (jouer)	After work I played squash with Jacques.
b.	Puis j'ai ...... avec ma femme. (dîner)	Then I had dinner with my wife.
c.	Après le dîner, j'ai ...... à mon collègue Jules. (téléphoner)	After dinner, I rang my colleague Jules.
d.	Nous avons ...... du nouveau projet. (discuter)	We discussed the new plan.
e.	Il m'a ...... de sa co-opération. (assurer)	He assured me of his co-operation.
f.	Nous avons ...... d'une date pour la conférence de presse. (décider)	We decided on a date for the press conference.
g.	Il m'a ...... la nouvelle plaquette produit par e-mail. (envoyer)	He sent me the new brochure by e-mail.

h. J'ai . . . . . . une page. (changer) — I changed a page.
i. Je l'ai . . . . (imprimer) — I printed it out.
j. Après ça, j'ai . . . . . . un feuilleton à la télévision. (regarder) — After that I watched a soap, on TV.

1.13.4 Irregular past participles

Many English past participles are irregular, but we are so used to them, that we don't notice.

run, ran, **run**; eat, ate, **eaten**; drink, drank, **drunk**

Some French verbs also have irregular past participles. Although there seem to be quite a lot, they are easy to learn, as they mostly follow the same patterns. These verbs all have past participles which end in **-u**.

infinitive	**past participle**	**example**	**meaning**
avoir	eu	Il a eu une surprise.	He had a surprise.
boire	bu	Nous avons bu du vin.	We have drunk some wine.
croire	cru	J'ai cru le reconnaître.	I thought I recognised him.
devoir	dû	Il a dû y aller.	He has had to go there.
lire	lu	Il a lu le livre.	He has read the book.
pouvoir	pu	Vous avez pu manger.	You were able to eat.
recevoir	reçu	Elle a reçu une lettre.	She has received a letter.
savoir	su	Ils ont su la réponse.	The knew the answer.
voir	vu	Il a vu l'accident.	He saw the accident.
vouloir	voulu	Nous avons voulu de l'eau.	We wanted some water.

The past participles of **prendre** (and verbs made up of **prendre**) and **mettre** end in **-s**.

infinitive	**past participle**	**example**	**meaning**
prendre	pris	Elle a pris son manteau.	She took her coat.
comprendre	compris	J'ai compris.	I've understood.
apprendre	appris	Elle a appris son nom.	She learned his name.
mettre	mis	Il a mis son imperméable.	He put on his raincoat.

The past participles of **faire**, **dire**, **écrire** end in **-t**.

infinitive	past participle	example	meaning
faire	fait	J'ai fait du sport.	I've done some sport.
dire	dit	Il m'a dit le nom de son amie.	He told me the name of his friend.
écrire	écrit	Elle a écrit une lettre.	She wrote a letter.

Some verbs don't follow a pattern.

infinitive	past participle	example	meaning
ouvrir	ouvert	Il a ouvert la fenêtre.	He opened the window.
être	été	J'ai été fatigué(e).	I have been tired.

Choose the five which you think you will need most and learn them.

V Complete these sentences by adding the past participle of the verb given in brackets.

a.	Notre client japonais a ...... la maquette du nouveau dépliant. (voir)	Our Japanese client has seen the new sample brochure.
b.	Alain a ...... les photos. (faire)	Alain did the photos.
c.	Nous avons ...... le texte. (écrire)	We wrote the text.
d.	Mme Brandt l'a ...... sur ordinateur. (mettre)	Mrs Brandt put it on the computer.
e.	La société de M. Patte l'a ...... en couleur. (imprimer)	Mr Patte's company printed it in colour.
f.	Avez-vous ...... les dernières épreuves? (voir)	Have you seen the latest proofs?
g.	Nous avons ...... en faire 5 000 exemplaires. (devoir)	We had to make 5,000 copies.
h.	Notre client a ...... satisfait. (être)	Our client was happy.

VI Now tell the story of Marcel's car. Complete these sentences using the perfect tense of the verb given in brackets. Not all the past participles are irregular!

a.	Marcel ...... 100 000 Euros au loto. (gagner)	Marcel won 100,000 Euros on the lottery.
b.	Il ...... acheter une nouvelle voiture pour sa femme. (vouloir)	He wanted to buy a new car for his wife.

c.	Il . . . . . . une pub pour une voiture éléctrique. (lire)	He read an advert for an electric car.
d.	Il . . . . . . la voiture. (acheter)	He bought the car.
e.	Sa femme n'a pas aimé la voiture et . . . . . . de la vendre. (décider)	His wife didn't like the car and decided to sell it.
f.	Elle . . . . . . un petit annonce sur le panneau d'affichage au supermarché. (mettre)	She put an advertisement on the notice board in the supermarket.
g.	L'ami de son mari . . . . . . un rendez-vous pour essayer la voiture. (prendre)	Her husband's friend made an appointment to try the car out.
h.	Marcel . . . . . . sa femme avec son ami dans la voiture. (voir)	Marcel saw his wife in the car with his friend.
i.	Il . . . . . . qu'ils avaient une liaison. (croire)	He thought they were having an affair.
j.	Il . . . . . . la voiture. (suivre)	He followed the car.
k.	Il . . . . . . des excès de vitesse. (faire)	He went too fast.
l.	Les gendarmes l'. . . . . . . (arrêter)	The policie stopped him.
m.	Il . . . . . . payer une amende. (devoir)	He had to pay a fine.

VII Can you translate these?

a. Stéphanie has read his latest novel (son dernier roman).
b. Have you read the book?
c. We haven't read the book.
d. They have seen the film.
e. Stéphanie saw the film yesterday.
f. We haven't seen the film.
g. Have you seen the film?
h. Stéphanie wrote a letter.
i. I haven't received a letter.
j. She posted it (mettre à la poste) yesterday.
k. Her husband took his umbrella.
l. He forgot his newspaper.
m. The haven't understood.
n. We understood.
o. I understood.

VIII Practice with 'avoir'. **How would you say . . .?**

a.	I have eaten	. . . mangé
b.	you have	
c.	we have	
d.	they have	
e.	he has	
f.	she has	
g.	you have	

h. John has
i. Have you?
j. my wife and I have

1.13.5 More on verbs which go with *être*

Remember, some verbs go with **être**. **Aller** is one of the ones you use most:

je suis allé(e) — nous sommes allé(e)s
tu es allé(e) — vous êtes allé(e)s
il/elle est allé(e) — ils/elles sont allé(e)s

IX Which form of être **would you use to complete these sentences?**

a. Nous . . . . . . allé(e)s en ville.
b. Je . . . . . . allé(e) au cinéma.
c. . . . . . .-vous allés au cinéma?
d. Mes collègues . . . . . . allés au théâtre.
e. Mon ami . . . . . . allé au concert.
f. Où . . . . . .-tu allé(e)?
g. Ma fille . . . . . . allée chez le dentiste.
h. Mes stagiaires . . . . . . sorties.
i. Où . . . . . .-vous allés?
j. Nous . . . . . . rentrés tard.

All the past participles of verbs that go with ***être*** *are regular except* ***naître*** *– to be born (****né****) (which you probably know already) and* ***mourir*** *– to die (****mort****) (which sounds like the beginning of mortuary).*

Reminder on how to form regular past participles
-er *verbs: take off the* ***-er*** *and add* ***-é***
-ir *verbs: take off the* ***-ir*** *and add* ***-i***
-re *verbs: take off the* ***-re*** *and add* ***-u***

X Complete these sentences by adding the past participle. What did Maurice do?

a. Marcel est . . . . . . à l'hôpital voir son père. (aller)
b. Il est . . . . . . de chez lui à neuf heures vingt. (sortir)
c. Le bus est . . . . . . à neuf heures et demie. (partir)
d. Il est . . . . . . à dix heures. (arriver)
e. Il est . . . . . . du bus devant l'hôpital. (descendre)
f. Il est . . . . . . dans l'hôpital. (entrer)
g. Il est . . . . . . au service cardiologie. (monter)
h. Il est . . . . . . dans l'escalier. (tomber)
i. Il est . . . . . . à l'hôpital. (rester)

XI This time add the correct form of être.

a. Céline . . . . . . allée à Paris voir ses parents.
b. Elle . . . . . . sortie de chez elle à neuf heures vingt.
c. Je . . . . . . allé(e) avec elle.
d. Le train . . . . . . parti à neuf heures et demie.
e. Nous . . . . . . arrivé(e)s à dix heures à la Gare du Nord.
f. Nous . . . . . . descendu(e)s du train.
g. Son frère . . . . . . venu la chercher à la gare.
h. Elle . . . . . . allée chez ses parents.
i. Je . . . . . . allé(e) au musée du Louvre.

1.13.6 Verbs with *être*: past participle agreement

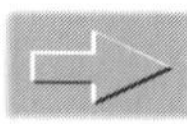

If you are not going to write in French go on to 1.13.7.

The past participle agrees with the subject (the person who is doing the action) by taking the following endings (which are not pronounced).

masculine	feminine	masculine plural	feminine plural
–	-e	-s	-es

XII Add endings to the past participles which need them.

a. Ma grand-mère est *né* en 1950.
b. Mon grand-père est *mort* l'année dernière.
c. Ma grand-mère est *allé* chez mes parents.
d. Elle est *parti* de la maison à onze heures.
e. Elle est *arrivé* à la gare à onze heures et demie.
f. Mes parents sont *allé* la chercher à la gare.
g. Le train est *arrivé* en retard.
h. Ma tante est *venu* la voir.
i. Elle est *monté* au grenier pour chercher de vieilles photos.
j. En descendant elle est *tombé* et s'est fait mal au genou.

XIII Now see if you can add the correct form: allé, allée, allés, allées.

a. M. Dupin est . . . . . . à Londres.
b. Son amie Charlotte est . . . . . . à Paris.
c. Ses parents sont . . . . . . sur la côte d'Azur.
d. Nous sommes . . . . . . en Bretagne.
e. Ses collègues sont . . . . . . en Espagne.
f. Vous êtes . . . . . . en Autriche.
g. Ses grands-parents sont . . . . . . en Italie.
h. Son meilleur ami est . . . . . . en Suisse.

i. Tu es . . . . . . aux États-Unis . . .
j. . . . et moi? Je suis . . . . . . à la maison!

Now see how many of the verbs which go with ***être*** *you can still remember, without looking. There were twelve of them! (See 1.13.1.)*

1.13.7 Reflexive verbs in the perfect tense

All reflexive verbs also go with **être**.

present	**perfect**
je me lève	je me suis levé(e)
tu te lèves	tu t'es levé(e)
il se lève	il s'est levé
elle se lève	elle s'est levée
nous nous levons	nous nous sommes levé(e)s
vous vous levez	vous vous êtes levé(e)s
ils se lèvent	ils se sont levés
elles se lèvent	elles se sont levées

At first you will probably only need to use reflexive verbs in the first person (I), so learn one phrase by heart and use it as a model to make other phrases later.

Je me suis couché(e) tard.	*I went to bed late.*
Je me suis bien débrouillé(e).	*I managed fine.*
Je me suis trompé(e) de route.	*I went the wrong way.*
Je me suis arrêté(e) au bord de la route.	*I stopped at the roadside.*

XIV For more practice with the other persons, see if you can give the right form of the perfect tense of se lever **to complete these sentences: When did they get up?**

a. Ce matin je . . . . . . à six heures.
b. Le boulanger . . . . . . à quatre heures.
c. Sa femme . . . . . . à quatre heures et demie.
d. Gilles . . . . . . à sept heures et demie.
e. Patrice et Monique . . . . . . à sept huit heures moins le quart.
f. Céline, à quelle heure tu . . . . . . ?
g. Nous . . . . . . à six heures.
h. M. et Mme Bériot . . . . . . à neuf heures.
i. Aurélie et Cécile . . . . . . à neuf heures et demie.
j. A quelle heure vous . . . . . . ce matin?

Here are some more reflexive verbs. You probably know most of them already.

infinitive	meaning	present tense	perfect tense
s'arrêter	to stop	je m'arrête	je me suis arrêté(e)
se coucher	to go to bed	je me couche	je me suis couché(e)
se débrouiller	to manage	je me débrouille	je me suis débrouillé(e)
s'égarer	to get lost	je m'égare	je me suis égaré(e)
s'endormir	to fall asleep	je m'endors	je me suis endormi(e)
s'énerver	to get impatient	je m'énerve	je me suis énervé(e)
s'intéresser	to be interested	je m'intéresse	je me suis intéressé(e)
se laver	to get washed	je me lave	je me suis lavé(e)
se moquer	to make fun of	je me moque	je me suis moqué(e)
se promener	to go for a walk	je me promène	je me suis promené(e)
se reposer	to rest	je me repose	je me suis reposé(e)
se réveiller	to wake up	je me réveille	je me suis réveillé(e)
se souvenir	to remember	je me souviens	je me suis souvenu(e)
se tromper	to be mistaken	je me trompe	je me suis trompé(e)

XV What did we do yesterday? Add the right part of the verb given in brackets.

a. Nous ...... à huit heures. (se réveiller)
b. Nous ...... à neuf heures. (se lever)
c. Nous ...... le long de la rivière. (se promener)
d. Nous ...... de route. (se tromper)
e. Nous .... (s'égarer)
f. Nous ...... dans un petit village. (s'arrêter)
g. Nous ...... un peu. (se reposer)
h. Mon amie .... (s'énerver)
i. Elle ...... d'un ami qui habite dans le coin. (se souvenir)
j. Elle est partie et je ...... tout seule. (se débrouiller)

1.13.8 Quickie

- You use the perfect tense to talk about something which has happened in the past.
- Most verbs form the perfect tense with *avoir* and the past participle of the verb: *j'ai mangé.*
- Some verbs (verbs of going and coming and reflexive verbs) form the perfect tense with *être*: *je suis allé(e).*
- In written French, the past participle of verbs with *être* has to agree with the subject.

1.14 The imperfect tense

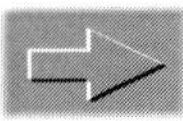

If you know when to use the imperfect tense, go to 1.14.1.

You use the imperfect tense to:

- describe what something was like in the past:

When I was small, we lived in Scotland.	Quand j'étais petit(e), nous habitions en Ecosse.
The house was old.	La maison était vieille.
It rained every day.	Il pleuvait tous les jours.

- say what someone or something used to do:

I used to walk to school.	J'allais à l'école à pied.
We used to collect wood for the fire.	Nous ramassions du bois pour le feu.
My father used to go fishing.	Mon père allait à la pêche.

- describe an interrupted action (say what someone/something was doing when something else happened):

I was watching (imperfect) television when the phone rang (perfect).	Je regardais la télévision quand le téléphone a sonné.

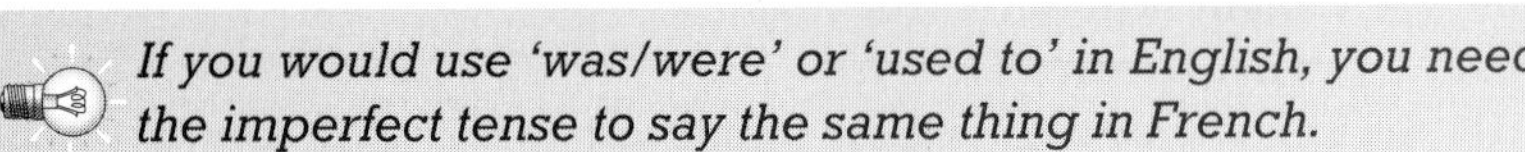

If you would use 'was/were' or 'used to' in English, you need to use the imperfect tense to say the same thing in French.

1.14.1 Formation of the imperfect tense

To form the imperfect tense, you need to know the **nous** form of the present tense, e.g. **nous parlons**, **nous dormons**, **nous finissons**, **nous répondons**. Then take off the **-ons** and add the following endings.

person	ending
je	-ais
tu	-ais
il/elle	-ait
nous	-ions
vous	-iez
ils/elles	-aient

1.14.2 Regular verbs

infinitive	nous form	imperfect
habiter	habitons	habitais
dormir finir	dormons finissons	dormais finissais
répondre	répondons	répondais

I Que faisaient-ils? **What were they doing when the lights went out?**

a. Mon mari ...... devant la télévision. (dormir)
b. Jean-Claude ...... la télévision. (regarder)
c. Mélanie ...... une revue. (lire)
d. Je ...... avec ma voisine. (discuter)
e. Nous ...... du nouveau premier ministre. (parler)
f. Sandrine ...... une douche. (prendre)
g. François ...... à sa petite amie. (téléphoner)
h. Laurence et son amie ...... sa moto dans le garage. (réparer)
i. Nicolas et Alexandre ...... au billard dans la salle de jeux. (jouer)

1.14.3 Irregular verbs

These verbs are irregular in the **nous** form of the present tense.

infinitive	nous form	imperfect
avoir être aller boire manger lire faire	avons êtes allons buvons mangeons lisons faisons	avais étions* allais buvais mangeais lisais faisais

* In written French note the change of accent in the imperfect of **être**.

II Give the correct form of avoir.

a. She was ten. — Elle ...... dix ans.
b. They were hungry. — Ils ...... faim.
c. We were thirsty. — Nous ...... soif.
d. You were late. — Vous ...... du retard.
e. I had a terrible headache. — J'...... un mal de tête affreux.

For expressions with **avoir** see 1.24.

III Now do the same with être.

a.	He was young.	Il . . . . . . jeune.
b.	They were pretty.	Ils . . . . . . beaux.
c.	You were magnificent.	Vous . . . . . . magnifique!
d.	It was sad.	C'. . . . . . triste.
e.	We were tired.	Nous . . . . . . fatigués.

IV Give the correct form of the imperfect of the verb in brackets.

a. J'. . . . . . à l'arrêt du bus. (attendre)
b. Tu . . . . . . McSolaar sur ton baladeur. (écouter)
c. Nous . . . . . . en ville. (aller)
d. Patrice . . . . . . son journal. (lire)
e. Il . . . . . . sa petite amie. (attendre)
f. Martin . . . . . . de chez lui. (sortir)
g. Ses parents . . . . . . à la campagne. (être)
h. Sylvie . . . . . . du jogging. (faire)
i. Vous . . . . . . la télévision. (regarder)
j. Mon père . . . . . . un apéritif. (boire)

V Complete the sentences by adding the correct form of the imperfect of the verb in brackets.

a. Il . . . . . . beau. (faire)
b. Il . . . . (neiger)*
c. Il y . . . . . . du soleil. (avoir)
d. Le vent . . . . (souffler)
e. Le soleil . . . . (briller)
f. Il . . . . (pleuvoir)
g. La brume . . . . (se dissiper)
h. Il . . . . . . chaud. (faire)
i. Il y . . . . . . un orage. (avoir)
j. La mer . . . . . . agitée. (être)

* In written French when **g** is followed by **a** or **o**, you need to add an **e** to keep the sound soft. (See Section 1.6.2.)

1.14.4 Perfect or imperfect?

Remember to use the imperfect tense for the action that was ongoing and the perfect tense for the action that 'interrupted' it.

VI You need to use both the imperfect and the perfect in these sentences.

a. Ses parents . . . . . . (habiter) à Nice quand Nadège . . . . . . (naître).
b. Quand elle . . . . . . (être) petite, sa famille . . . . . . (déménager) à Paris.

c. Elle . . . . . . (avoir) cinq ans quand son frère . . . . . . (naître).
d. Il . . . . . . (avoir) un accident quand il . . . . . . (avoir) dix ans.
e. Il . . . . . . (traverser) la rue quand une voiture . . . . . . (griller) le feu rouge.
f. Nadège . . . . . . (voir) l'accident pendant qu'elle . . . . . . (attendre) le bus.
g. Elle . . . . . . (avoir) dix-neuf ans quand elle . . . . . . (passer) son bac.
h. Elle . . . . . . (faire) des études de biologie quand elle . . . . . . (décider) de quitter l'université.
i. Elle . . . . . . (suivre) un cours de dactylo quand elle . . . . . . (voir) l'annonce de Megasoc.
j. Elle . . . . . . (travailler) dans la société quand elle . . . . . . (rencontrer) son futur mari.
k. Elle . . . . . . (être) chef du personnel quand il . . . . . . (poser) sa candidature.
l. Il . . . . . . (faire) beau quand ils . . . . . . (se marier).

1.14.5 Quickie

- The imperfect tense is easy as it is always formed in the same way.
- Take the *nous* form of the verb in the present tense, remove the *-ons* and add the new endings. The endings are the same for all verbs, and only the *nous* and *vous* forms sound different: *-ais*, *-ais*, *-ait*, *-ions*, *-iez*, *-aient*.
- You are most likely to need to use the imperfect tense when talking about yourself . . .
- . . . or about the weather: *il faisait*, *il y avait*, etc.

VII How would you say the following?
a. When I was young . . .
b. When I was waiting at the bus stop . . .
c. It was raining.
d. It was cold.
e. It was sunny.

1.15 The future tense

You use the future tense to talk about something that is going to happen, something you want to do or are going to do in the future. In French, just as in English, there are two ways of saying what is going to happern.

1.15.1 *Futur proche* or near future

This is like the English *I am going to . . .*, e.g. *I am going to go*, *He is going to play*, and is made up of **aller** (*to go*) and the main verb, just as it is in English.

Je vais sortir. I am going to go out.

This is the most useful future tense to learn as it is used most frequently in conversation, when talking about the near future: this evening, tomorrow, in the next few days.

To make the **futur proche**, you need to know the present tense of the verb **aller** and the infinitive of the verb you want to use.

aller

singular	meaning	plural	meaning
je vais tu vas il/elle va	I am going you are going he/she is going	nous allons vous allez ils/elles vont	we are going you are going they are going

Je vais dîner au restaurant.	I am going to eat in the restaurant.
Tu vas regarder l'émission.	You are going to watch the programme.
Il va arriver en retard.	He is going to arrive late.
Nous allons déjeuner.	We are going to have breakfast.
Vous allez visiter le musée.	You are going to visit the museum.
Ils vont faire du ski.	They are going to go skiing.

I What are these people going to do? Complete the sentences by adding the correct form of the verb aller.

a. Je ...... faire de la planche à voile.
b. Tu ...... faire du parapente.
c. Maurice ...... faire du rafting.
d. Nous ...... faire du VTT.
e. Vous ...... faire du ski de fond.
f. Nathalie et Simon ...... faire du surf de neige.
g. Vous ...... faire du canyoning?
h. Patrice et Benjamin ...... faire de l'escalade.
i. Je ...... rester à la maison.

II L'anniversaire de Cally McGael. **What are they going to do for Cally's birthday? Add the missing part of** aller.

a. Ses collègues ...... organiser une fête.
b. Thomas ...... faire un gâteau.
c. Barbara ...... envoyer les invitations.
d. Cass et Col ...... préparer le repas.
e. Ben ...... acheter du champagne.
f. Son chef ...... lui offrir un cadeau.
g. Norman ...... décorer la pièce.
h. Nous ...... aider Norman.
i. Mike ...... chercher des verres.
j. Vous ...... chanter 'bon anniversaire'.

1.15.2 The *futur*

This is the 'proper' future tense. It translates the English *will* and can imply intention as well as future action.

je jouerai	I will play
il ira	he will go
ils écouteront	they will listen

If you have had enough of tenses just learn the ***je*** *form and go on to 1.15.3.*

Fortunately, most verbs are regular! The **futur** is made by adding these endings to the infinitive: **-ai**, **-as**, **-a**, **-ons**, **-ez**, **-ont**. If the infinitive ends in **-e**, take the **-e** off first.

-er verbs	-ir verbs	-re verbs
je parlerai tu parleras il/elle parlera nous parlerons vous parlerez ils/elles parleront	**je finirai** tu finiras il/elle finira nous finirons vous finirez ils/elles finiront	**je répondrai** tu répondras il/elle répondra nous répondrons vous répondrez ils/elles répondront

III Give the correct future tense of the verbs in brackets.

a. nous . . . . . . (regarder)
b. tu . . . . . . (préparer)
c. vous . . . . . . (mettre)
d. ils . . . . . . (manger)
e. il . . . . . . (prendre)
f. vous . . . . . . (sortir)
g. elles . . . . . . (arriver)
h. nous . . . . . . (entrer)
i. je . . . . . . (partir)
j. elle . . . . . . (porter)

IV Que porteront-ils? **What are they going to wear for the mardi-gras carnival?**

a. Je . . . . . . le costume traditionnel.
b. Juliette . . . . . . une jupe fleurie et une blouse blanche.
c. Mon ami . . . . . . son tailleur noir et une écharpe blanche.
d. Nicolas . . . . . . son jean délavé et un vieux tee-shirt, comme toujours.
e. Mes amies . . . . . . les robes traditionelles brodées.
f. Mes amis . . . . . . un pantalon noir et une chemise blanche.
g. Nous . . . . . . des chaussettes blanches et les chaussures noires.
h. Que . . . . . .-vous?

1.15.3 Irregular verbs

Some of the most common verbs are irregular in the future tense.

Look for patterns to help you remember them and choose the four that you think you are most likely to need, and learn the ***je*** *form of them.*

infinitive	**future**
être	je serai, tu seras, . . .
avoir	j'aurai, tu auras, . . .
aller	j'irai, tu iras, . . .
faire	je ferai, tu feras, . . .
devoir	je devrai, tu devras, . . .
pouvoir	je pourrai, tu pourras, . . .
savoir	je saurai, tu sauras, . . .
voir	je verrai, tu verras, . . .
vouloir	je voudrai, tu voudras, . . .
falloir	il faudra
venir	je viendrai, tu viendras, . . .
tenir	je tiendrai, tu tiendras, . . .

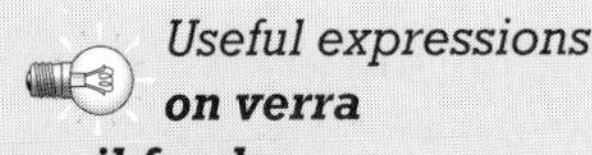

Useful expressions:

on verra — *we will see*

il faudra — *it will be necessary*

V For more practice give the correct form of the verb in brackets.

a. j'. . . . . . (aller)
b. vous . . . . . . (venir)
c. tu . . . . . . (faire)
d. nous . . . . . . (avoir)
e. il . . . . . . (être)
f. elle . . . . . . (voir)
g. ils . . . . . . (vouloir)
h. nous . . . . . . (devoir)
i. vous . . . . . . (savoir)
j. elles . . . . . . (tenir)
k. il . . . . . . (falloir)
l. vous . . . . . . (pouvoir)

VI Ils vont dans les Alpes. **Add the correct form of the verb in brackets.**

a. Nous . . . . . . après-demain. (partir)
b. Le taxi . . . . . . à cinq heures. (arriver)

c. Nous . . . . . . le vol de huit heures trente. (prendre)
d. Il y . . . . . . un bus pour faire le trajet de l'aéroport à la station de ski. (avoir)
e. Tout le monde . . . . . . du ski. (faire)
f. A midi, nous . . . . . . au châlet. (déjeuner)
g. On . . . . . . le soir. (sortir)
h. Il . . . . . . froid. (faire)
i. Nous . . . . . . porter des vêtements chauds. (devoir)

1.16 The conditional tense

The conditional tense is used to translate *would* in English. It is called the conditional because you are making a condition: I would go if you paid me! But it is also used to be more polite: I would like a box of chocolates.

1.16.1 Formation of the conditional

It is easy to learn, as it is just like the future but it has slightly different endings: **-ais**, **-ais**, **-ait**, **-ions**, **-iez**, **-aient**.

-er verbs	-ir verbs	-re verbs
je jouerais tu jouerais il/elle jouerait nous jouerions vous joueriez ils/elles joueraient	je finirais tu finirais il/elle finirait nous finirions vous finiriez ils/elles finiraient	je répondrais tu répondrais il/elle répondrait nous répondrions vous répondriez il/elles répondraient

I How would you say the following?

I would . . .
a. eat (manger)
b. drink (boire)
c. sleep (dormir)
d. speak (parler)
e. live (habiter)
f. buy (acheter)
g. ask (demander)
h. listen (écouter)
i. watch (regarder)

II Add the right part of jouer **to the following.**
a. I would play tennis. Je . . . . . . au tennis.
b. My friend would play too. Mon amie . . . . . . aussi.

c.	Her friends would play too.	Ses amies . . . . . . aussi.
d.	We wouldn't play.	Nous ne . . . . . . pas.
e.	You would play football.	Vous . . . . . . au foot.

III Add the right part of préférer **to these sentences.**

a.	I would prefer to go to the beach.	Je . . . . . . aller à la plage.
b.	My boyfriend would prefer to go windsurfing.	Mon petit ami . . . . . . faire de la planche à voile.
c.	My girlfriends would prefer to go to town.	Mes amies . . . . . . aller en ville.
d.	We would prefer to eat in a restaurant.	Nous . . . . . . manger au restaurant.
e.	What would you prefer?	Que . . . . . .-vous?

IV Now add the right part of aimer.

a.	I would like to go out.	J'. . . . . . sortir.
b.	Gilles would like to stay in.	Gilles . . . . . . rester à la maison.
c.	Patrice would like to go to the cinema.	Patrice . . . . . . aller au cinéma.
d.	My parents would like to go to America.	Mes parents . . . . . . aller aux États-Unis.
e.	What would you like to do?	Qu'est-ce que vous . . . . . . faire?

1.16.2 Irregular verbs

These are just the same as in the future, but with the new endings.

infinitive	conditional	meanings
être	je serais	I would be
avoir	j'aurais	I would have
aller	j'irais	I would go
faire	je ferais	I would do
devoir	je devrais	I ought to
pouvoir	je pourrais	I could
savoir	je saurais	I would know
voir	je verrais	I would see
vouloir	je voudrais	I would like
falloir	il faudrait	It would be necessary
tenir	je tiendrais	I would hold
venir	je viendrais	I would come

V Talking about yourself: how would you say the following?

a.	I would like a baguette.	Je . . . . . . une baguette. (vouloir)
b.	I would go to town.	J'. . . . . . en ville. (aller)
c.	I would have a friend.	J'. . . . . . un ami. (avoir)
d.	I would see my friends.	Je . . . . . . mes amis. (voir)
e.	I would go to France.	J'. . . . . . en France. (aller)
f.	I would go windsurfing.	Je . . . . . . faire de la planche à voile. (pouvoir)
g.	I would be happy.	Je . . . . . . heureux/heureuse. (être)
h.	I would know the answer.	Je . . . . . . la réponse. (savoir)
i.	I would have to go out.	Je . . . . . . sortir. (devoir)
j.	I would hold his hand.	Je lui . . . . . . la main. (tenir)

VI What could they do? Fill in the correct form of pouvoir**.**

a.	Nicole could go home.	Nicole . . . . . . rentrer chez elle.
b.	We could go to the cinema.	Nous . . . . . . aller au cinéma.
c.	We could go to the leisure centre.	Nous . . . . . . aller au centre de loisirs.
d.	I could do judo.	Je . . . . . . faire du judo.
e.	You could play volleyball.	Vous . . . . . . jouer au volleyball.
f.	Camille could go riding.	Camille . . . . . . faire du cheval.
g.	The children could go swimming.	Les enfants . . . . . . aller à la piscine.
h.	We could meet afterwards.	Nous . . . . . . se retrouver après.
i.	We could go to McDonalds.	Nous . . . . . . aller chez McDo.
j.	We could go back to my house.	Nous . . . . . . rentrer chez moi.

1.16.3 Quickie

- The conditional translates *would*, e.g. *I would go*, *I would like*.
- You probably already know *je voudrais* (*I would like*), so you already know the ending.
- Remember that the endings for *je/tu/il/elle/on* and *ils/elles* all sound the same, so you just have to remember the *-ions* and *-iez* endings for *nous* and *vous*.
- The most useful conditionals are:

je voudrais	I would like
j'aimerais	I would like
je préférerais	I would prefer
on pourrait	one/we could
on devrait	one/we should
il faudrait	it would be necessary

1.17 The subjunctive

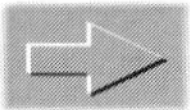

If you are not ready for the subjunctive yet go on to 1.17.3.

The subjunctive is not used much in English any more (only in expressions such as *If I were you . . .*), but it is still used in certain expressions in French. It is useful to be able to recognise it when you hear it. Try to learn one or two of the expressions by heart and then use them as a model, or find out how to avoid expressions which need the subjunctive and go on to 1.18!

In French, the subjunctive is used after verbs expressing a wish or desire . . .

I would like him to go.	J'aimerais qu'il parte.
I wish him to come.	Je voudrais qu'il vienne.

. . . or a requirement (after **il faut que** (*it is necessary that*)) . . .

He must be able to drive.	Il faut qu'il sache conduire.

. . . and after certain fixed expressions.

in order to	afin que
although	bien que
before	avant que
until	jusqu'à ce que

1.17.1 Formation of the subjunctive

The subjunctive is formed by taking the **ils** form of the present tense, removing the **-ent** and then adding these endings: **-e**, **-es**, **-e**, **-ions**, **-iez**, **-ent**. Fortunately, in regular **-er** verbs (and therefore most verbs), in most persons it sounds just like the present, so you can't tell whether you are using it or not. Unfortunately, the verbs you use most are irregular. Even if you do not want to learn them, you should be able to recognise them.

Regular verbs

porter	finir	formir	répondre
je porte tu portes il/elle porte nous portions vous portiez ils/elles portent	je finisse tu finisses il/elle finisse nous finissions vous finissiez ils/elles finissent	je dorme tu dormes il/elle dorme nous dormions vous dormiez ils/elles dorment	je réponde tu répondes il/elle réponde nous répondions vous répondiez ils/elles répondent

Irregular verbs

The most useful irregular verbs are:

aller	avoir	être	faire	pouvoir	savoir	vouloir
j'aille	j'aie	je sois	je fasse	je puisse	je sache	je veuille
tu ailles	tu aies	tu sois	tu fasses	tu puisses	tu saches	tu veuilles
il/elle aille	il/elle ait	il/elle soit	il/elle fasse	il/elle puisse	il/elle sache	il/elle veuille
nous aillions	nous ayons	nous soyons	nous fassions	nous puissions	nous sachions	nous veuillions
vous ailliez	vous ayez	vous soyez	vous fassiez	vous puissiez	vous sachiez	vous veuilliez
ils/elles aillent	ils/elles aient	ils/elles soient	ils/elles fassent	ils/elles puissent	ils/elles sachent	ils/elles veuillent

1.17.2 Expressions which take the subjunctive

Expressions of necessity

Il faut que je parte. — I have to go.
Il est nécessaire qu'elle sache. — She has to know.

Wishes or preferences

Je veux qu'il soit à l'heure. — I want him to be on time.
Il préfère que j'y aille. — He prefers me to go (there).

Possibility

Il est possible qu'il puisse venir. — It is possible that he can come.
Il est impossible qu'il soit en retard. — It is not possible for him to be late.

Doubt and disbelief

Je ne crois pas qu'il soit malade. — I don't believe that he is ill.
Je doute qu'il fasse très froid. — I don't think that it will be very cold.

Regret

Je regrette qu'il ait été blessé. — I am sorry that he has been hurt.
Je suis désolé(e) que vous ne puissiez venir. — I am sorry that you can't come.

Bien que – although

Bien que vous soyez malade, vous devez vous présenter au tribunal. — Although you are ill, you have to go to court.

1.17.3 Recognising the subjunctive

Even if you do not feel ready to use the subjunctive yet, it is useful to be able to recognise when you hear it.

I Which verb is being used? Read the sentence and work out the infinitive of the word in italics.

a.	Il faut qu'il *vienne.*	He must come.
b.	Je ne crois pas qu'il *prenne* le bus.	I don't believe he'll come by bus.
c.	Je regrette qu'il ne *fasse* pas beau aujourd'hui.	I'm sorry that it's not fine today.
d.	*Soyez* le bienvenue!	Welcome!
e.	Il est possible qu'ils *aient* oublié.	It's possible that they might have forgotten.
f.	Bien qu'elle *ait* une voiture, elle préfère prendre le métro.	Although she has a car, she prefers to take the tube.

1.18 Other tenses

Just when you think you have learned all the tenses, you pick up a book or a newspaper and find that there are even more. Fortunately, you don't have to learn to use them to speak good French, but it is a good idea to be able to recognise them. Here are two more.

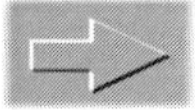

If you don't need them yet go on to 1.19.

1.18.1 The pluperfect tense

This translates the English *I had done something when . . .* It is formed in the same way in French as in English, i.e. it is the same as the perfect tense but with the imperfect form of **avoir** or **être**.

perfect		**pluperfect**	
j'ai mangé	I have eaten	j'avais mangé	I had eaten
je suis allé(e)	I went	j'étais allé(e)	I had been

1.18.2 The past historic

This tense is used in written French in narration, when writing about events that happened in the past. You will find it in some books, novels and newspapers. It is usually used in the third person.

Quand Sybille remonta chez elle, vers onze heures du soir, elle entendit de loin la guitare. Elle trouva le musicien assis sous un arbre dans le jardin. Elle ne le reconnaissa pas jusqu'à ce qu'il . . .

When Sybille made her way home at about eleven o'clock at night, she heard the distant sound of a guitar. She found the musician seated under a tree in the garden. She did not recognise him until he . . .

These are the past-historic endings.

travailler	finir	vendre
je travaillai tu travaillas il/elle travailla nous travaillâmes vous travaillâtes ils/elles travaillèrent	je finis tu finis il/elle finit nous finîmes vous finîtes ils/elles finirent	je vendis tu vendis il/elle vendit nous vendîmes vous vendîtes ils/elles vendirent

For a full list of tenses, see the verb tables page 148.

1.19 Imperatives

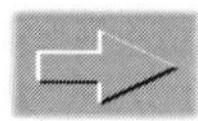

If you remember how to give orders and instructions go on to 1.20.

The imperative is the part of the verb you use when you are telling someone to do something, or giving instructions or an order: *Watch out! Stop! Turn left!* etc.

When you use the imperative you usually use the **vous** part of the verb. You use the **tu** form only when speaking to someone you know well or someone much younger than you.

Look at these examples. You will probably have heard some of these before. Which ones do you know already?

Come on!	Venez!
Go!	Allez!
Cross the road!	Traversez la rue!
Turn left!	Tournez à gauche!
Listen!	Ecoutez!
Wait!	Attendez!
Hold on (telephone).	Ne quittez pas.
Wait (telephone).	Patientez.
Hurry up!	Dépechez-vous!

1.19.1 Formation of the imperative

Vous form

To make the imperative, you use the **vous** form of the verb without the **vous**.

Tu form

You use the **tu** form of the verb, but **-er** verbs lose the final **-s** (but as it isn't pronounced, it sounds the same). Remember that you may only use the **tu** form to a child or someone you know really well who has asked you to **tutoyer**.

I How would you give these instructions? If you are likely to need to use the tu **form (**Mange les légumes! Va au lit!**) practise both forms; otherwise concentrate on the** vous **form.**

- **a.** ...... à gauche! (tourner)
- **b.** ...... les marches! (monter)
- **c.** ...... la première rue à gauche! (prendre)
- **d.** ...... tout droit. (continuer)
- **e.** ...... jusqu'aux prochains feux. (aller)
- **f.** ...... à droite et à gauche! (regarder)
- **g.** ...... la rue! (traverser)
- **h.** ...... le bus. (prendre)
- **i.** ...... devant le théâtre. (descendre)

II These instructions are from a soufflé recipe. Put them in the vous **form.**

- **a.** Pre-heat the oven. ...... le four. (préchauffer)
- **b.** Chop the onions. ...... l'oignon. (émincer)
- **c.** Beat the eggs. ...... les œufs. (battre)
- **d.** Put the onion into a bowl. ...... l'oignon dans un saladier. (mettre)
- **e.** Add the oil and the beaten eggs. ...... l'huile et les œufs battus. (ajouter)
- **f.** Mix well. ...... bien. (mélanger)
- **g.** Butter an oven-proof dish. ...... un moule. (beurrer)
- **h.** Pour the mixture into the dish. ...... le mélange dans le moule. (verser)
- **i.** Put the dish into the oven. ...... le moule au four. (mettre)
- **j.** Cook for ten minutes. ...... pendant dix minutes. (faire cuire)

III How would you tell someone to do these things? Use the vous **form.**

- **a.** Watch less television. ...... moins la télévision. (regarder)
- **b.** Eat more vegetables. ...... plus de légumes. (manger)
- **c.** Drink more water. ...... plus d'eau. (boire)
- **d.** Go jogging. ...... du jogging. (faire)
- **e.** Close the door. ...... la porte. (fermer)
- **f.** Open the window. ...... la fenêtre. (ouvrir)
- **g.** Show your passport. ...... votre passeport. (présenter)
- **h.** Speak more slowly. ...... plus lentement. (parler)
- **i.** Come with me. ...... avec moi. (venir)

1.20 Negative expressions

Negative statements include saying what you don't do, and expressions with *no*, *nothing*, *never*, *nobody*, etc.

1.20.1 How to say you don't do something

You already know to put **ne** in front of the verb and **pas** after the verb.

I don't know.	Je ne sais pas.
I don't speak French.	Je ne parle pas français.
I don't eat meat.	Je ne mange pas de viande.
He doesn't drink wine.	Il ne boit pas de vin.
They don't live in Paris.	Ils n'habitent pas à Paris.
You aren't married?	Vous n'êtes pas marié(e)?

1.20.2 Some more negative expressions

ne . . . plus — *no longer/more*
Nous n'allons plus en ville. — We don't go to town any more.

ne . . . que — *only*
Il ne boit que du coca. — He only drinks coca cola.

ne . . . jamais — *never*
Elle n'est jamais allée à Paris. — She has never been to Paris.

ne . . . rien — *nothing/not anything*
Je n'ai rien fait. — I didn't do anything.

ne . . . personne — *nobody/no one*
Il n'a vu personne. — He didn't see anyone.

I How would you say the following? If possible, say them aloud so that you can get used to the sound of them. Then cover up the English, read them again and think about the meaning. Finally cover up the French and translate the whole sentence.

a.	I have never been to France.	Je . . . . . . suis . . . . . . allé(e) en France.
b.	He has never seen Frédéric.	Il . . . . . .a . . . . . . vu Frédéric.
c.	We have never eaten in a restaurant.	Nous . . . . . .avons . . . . . . dîné au restaurant.
d.	They have never eaten meat.	Il . . . . . .ont . . . . . . mangé de viande.
e.	You have never learned to swim?	Vous . . . . . .avez . . . . . . appris à nager?
f.	I don't see Aline any more.	Je . . . . . . vois . . . . . . Aline.
g.	She doesn't ride a bike any more.	Elle . . . . . . fait . . . . . . de vélo.
h.	They don't live in Paris any longer.	Ils . . . . . .habitent . . . . . . Paris.
i.	He doesn't listen to his wife any more.	Il . . . . . .écoute . . . . . . sa femme.

j.	They don't have any more money.	Ils . . . . . .ont . . . . . . d'argent.
k.	I don't see anybody.	Je . . . . . . vois . . . .
l.	I didn't see anybody.	Je . . . . . .ai vu . . . .
m.	Jean-Luc saw nobody.	Jean-Luc . . . . . .a vu . . . .
n.	Nobody saw Jean-Luc.	. . . . .a vu Jean-Luc.
o.	They didn't hurt anyone.	Ils . . . . . .ont fait de mal à . . . .
p	I have only ten Euros left.	Il . . . . . . me reste . . . . . . dix Euros.
q.	They only have a small house.	Ils . . . . . .ont . . . . . .une petite maison.
v.	There is only one bedroom.	Il . . . . . .y a . . . . . .une chambre.
s.	Mr. Bériot only has one son.	M. Bériot . . . . . .a . . . . . .un fils.
t.	We only have a black and white printer.	Nous . . . . . .avons . . . . . .une imprimante noir et blanc.
u.	I don't have anything.	Je . . . . . .ai . . . .
v.	They haven't seen anything.	Ils . . . . . .ont . . . . . . vu.
w.	We didn't hear anything.	Nous . . . . . .avons . . . . . . entendu.
x.	You do nothing!	Vous . . . . . . faites . . . . . . !
y.	They never did anything.	Ils . . . . . .ont . . . . .fait!

II Match up these sentences.

a.	We haven't anything to eat.	Je n'avais pas le temps d'aller en ville.
b.	Nobody has been shopping.	Il n'y a que du pain et du fromage.
c.	I didn't have time to go to town.	Je n'ai plus d'argent.
d.	There is only some bread and cheese.	Nous n'avons rien à manger.
e.	You never go to the supermarket.	Vous n'allez jamais au supermarché.
f.	I haven't any more money.	Personne n'a fait les courses.

*Remember to use **de** to replace **du/de la/des** after negative expressions.*

1.21 Interrogatives

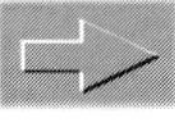

If you remember how to ask questions go on to 1.21.4.

There are three ways of asking a question:

- you can make a statement and change the intonation;
- you can invert the subject and the verb;
- you can use a question word, and then invert the subject and the verb.

In the following sections, read the examples and then cover up the English and see if you understand the meanings; then cover up the French and see if you can put them back into French.

1.21.1 Changing the intonation

This is the most colloquial way to ask a question, but if in doubt, you can always fall back on it.

Remember that the voice rises at the end of the question and falls at the end of a statement.

Vous comprenez?	You understand?
Vous parlez anglais?	You speak English?
Vous connaissez l'hôtel Superbe?	You know the Hotel Superbe?
Ce train va à Rouen?	This train is going to Rouen?

1.21.2 Inverting the subject and the verb

Comprenez-vous?	Do you understand?
Parlez-vous anglais?	Do you speak English?
Connaissez-vous l'hôtel Superbe?	Do you know the Hotel Superbe?
Ce train, va-t-il à Rouen?	Is this train going to Rouen?

Notice that in the third person, if the verb ends in a vowel, you have to add **-t**.

Joue-t-elle au tennis?	Does she play tennis?
A-t-il une nouvelle voiture?	Has he got a new car?

1.21.3 Using a question word

Où allez-vous?	Where are you going?
Comment va-t-il à Paris?	How is he going to Paris?
Pourquoi est-elle à Paris?	Why is she in Paris?
Quand partez-vous?	When are you learning?
Que faites-vous?	What are you doing?
Qui connaissez-vous?	Who do you know?
Combien de chambres avez-vous?	How many bedrooms do you have?

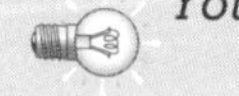

*You use **qui** (who?) for people and **que** (what?) for things.*

1.21.4 Which?

Quel is really an adjective, as it goes together with a noun and therefore has to agree with it (though its different forms mostly sound the same): **quel**, **quelle**, **quels**, **quelles**.

Quel CD cherche-t-il?	Which CD is he looking for?
Quelle saison préférez-vous?	Which season do you prefer?
Quels musiciens préférez-vous?	Which musicians do you prefer?
Quelles chanteuses préférez-vous?	Which (female) singers do you prefer?

I Which form of quel **would you use in the following?**

a.	Which author do you prefer?	...... écrivain préférez-vous?
b.	Which films do you prefer?	...... films préférez-vous?
c.	Which programmes do you prefer?	...... émissions préférez-vous?
d.	Which actress do you prefer?	...... actrice préférez-vous?

1.21.5 Est-ce que . . .

You can use **est-ce que** and then you don't need to invert the subject and the verb.

Où est-ce que vous allez?	Where are you going?
Comment est-ce qu'il va à Paris?	How is he going to Paris?
Pourquoi est-ce que vous allez à Paris?	Why are you going to Paris?
Quand est-ce que je dois partir?	When do I have to leave?
Qu'est-ce qu'il fait?	What is he doing?
Qui est-ce que vous connaissez déjà?	Who do you know already?
Combien de chambres est-ce qu'il y a?	How many rooms are there?

1.22 Expressions of time

In these expressions, you use a different tense in French from the one you would expect to use in English.

1.22.1 *Depuis* – since

In English, when we want to say we have been doing something for a certain length of time, we use the past tense. In French, they say they have been doing it since (a year etc.) and still are, so they use the present tense.

J'habite ici depuis six ans.	I have lived here for six years.
Il apprend le français depuis deux ans.	He has been learning French for two years.
J'ai cette voiture depuis un an.	I have had this car a year.
Ils attendent depuis une heure.	They have been waiting an hour.
Je suis ici depuis deux jours.	I have been here two days.

I How would you answer these questions (remember to use the present tense)?

a. Depuis quand habitez-vous ici?
b. Depuis combien de temps apprenez-vous le français?
c. Depuis combien de temps connaissez-vous votre meilleur ami/votre meilleure amie?

1.22.2 *Venir de* – to have just

Instead of using the past tense and saying *I have just seen him*, in French you use the verb **venir** and say *I come from seeing him.*

Present tense

Je viens de rentrer.	I have just got in.
Il vient de téléphoner.	He has just rung.
Nous venons de voir un film épouvantable.	We have just seen a dreadful film.

Imperfect tense

Je venais de rentrer quand . . .	I had just got in when . . .
Il venait de téléphoner quand . . .	He had just rung when . . .
Nous venions de voir ce film épouvantable quand . . .	We had just seen this dreadful film when . . .

1.22.3 When and the future

If you are talking about two things which will happen in the future, one depending on the other, both statements have to be in the future in French.

Quand il neigera, nous irons faire du ski.	When it snows, we will go skiing. (When it will snow, we will . . .)
Quand il fera beau, nous jouerons au tennis.	When it's fine, we will play tennis.
Quand je serai vieux/vieille j'irai vivre au bord de la mer.	When I am old, I am going to live by the sea. (When I will be old, I will live by the sea.)

1.23 Quickie tenses

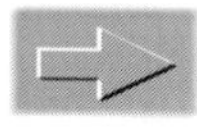

If you know when to use the different tenses, go on to 1.24.

Present tense

You use the present tense to talk about what is happening now . . .

Je lis	I am reading

. . . and to express generalisations.

Je ne regarde pas 'X-Files'. — I don't watch the X-Files.

These are the question forms.

Lisez-vous le journal? — Are you reading the paper?
Regardez-vous . . . ? — Do you watch . . . ?

Perfect tense

You use the perfect tense to talk about what has happened in the past.

J'ai joué au tennis. — I played tennis.
J'ai essayé. — I have tried.

These are the question forms.

Avez-vous joué? — Have you played?
Avez-vous essayé? — Did you try?

Imperfect tense

You use the imperfect tense to talk about what has happened in the past if:

- it was a habitual action;

  Je jouais quand j'étais petit(e). — I used to play (when I was young).
- it was an ongoing and interrupted action.

  Je regardais la télévision quand j'ai entendu les nouvelles de . . . — I was watching television when I heard the news about . . .

These are the question forms.

Jouiez-vous . . . ? — Did you used to play . . . ?
Regardiez-vous la télévision quand . . . ? — Were you watching television when . . . ?

Near future

You use the near future or **futur proche** to translate what you are about to do.

Je vais aller. — I am going to go.
Il va partir. — He is going to leave.

These are the question forms.

Allez-vous aller? — Are you going to go?
Va-t-il partir? — Is he going to leave?

Future

The future tense is used to express intention of what you are going to do in the future.

Je rangerai mon bureau la semaine prochaine. — I will tidy my office next week.
Quand nous irons en France j'irai voir . . . — When we (will) go to France, I will go and see . . .

These are the question forms.

Que ferez-vous? — What will you do?
Quand partirez-vous? — When will you go?

Imperative

The imperative is used to give orders or instructions.

Allez chercher mes pantoufles!	Fetch me my slippers!
Fermez la porte!	Shut the door!

Interrogative

The interrogative is used to ask questions.

Avez-vous . . . ?	Have you got a . . . ?
Avez-vous vu . . . ?	Did you see . . . ?

Conditional

The conditional is used to put things more politely . . .

Je voudrais . . .	I would like . . .
Pourriez-vous m'aider?	Could you help me?

. . . or to express conditions.

Je vous achéterais un cadeau si j'avais assez d'argent.	I would buy you a present if I had enough money.

Recognising a verb

*If a word that you don't know comes after a noun, the name of a person or after a pronoun (**je, tu, il/elle, nous, vous, ils/elles**), it is probably a verb.*

- *If it ends in **-e, -es, -ons, -ez, -ent, -s, -t**, or **-ont**, it is probably a verb in the present tense.*
- *If it ends in **-rai, -ras, -ra, -rons, -rez** or **-ront**, it is probably a verb in the future.*
- *If it comes after a part of **avoir** or **être** and ends with **é(e/s), u(e/s)** or **i(e/s)**, it is probably the past participle of a verb.*
- *If it ends in **-ais, -ait, -ions, -iez** or **-aient**, it is probably the imperfect tense of a verb.*
- *If it ends in **-rais, -rait, -rions, -riez** or **-raient**, it is probably the conditional of a verb.*

1.24 Special uses of *avoir*

Avoir is used in some expressions where *have* is not used in English. Here are some examples.

1.24.1 Age

You use **avoir** to say how old you are.

J'ai trente ans.	I am 30. (I have 30 years.)
Quel âge as-tu?	How old are you? (What age have you?)

Il a dix ans. — He is ten. (He has ten years.)
Nous avons 29 et 30 ans. — We are 29 and 30 years old. (We have 29 and 30 years.)
Vous avez quel âge? — How old are you? (What age have you?)
Ils ont 50 ans. — They are 50. (They have 50 years.)

Now say how old you are: **J'ai . . . ans.**

1.24.2 Saying what you need

avoir besoin de = *to need*

J'ai besoin d'un marteau. — I need a hammer.
As-tu besoin d'aide? — Do you need help?
Il a besoin de dormir. — He needs to sleep.
Nous avons besoin d'argent. — We need some money.
Avez-vous besoin de nous? — Do you need us?
Ils ont besoin d'une plus grande maison. — They need a bigger house.

1.24.3 Expressing fear

avoir peur de = *to be afraid of*

J'ai peur des hauteurs. — I am afraid of heights.
As-tu le vertige? — Do you suffer from vertigo?
Elle a peur des araignées. — She is afraid of spiders.
Nous avons peur de l'orage. — We are afraid of storms.
Avez-vous peur des fantômes? — Are you afraid of ghosts?
Ils ont peur des voyous. — They are afraid of hooligans.

1.24.4 Expressing cold and heat

avoir froid/chaud = *to be cold/hot*

J'ai froid. — I am cold.
As-tu froid? — Are you cold?
Il a froid. — He is cold.
Nous avons chaud. — We are hot.
Avez-vous trop chaud? — Are you too hot?
Ils ont chaud. — They are hot.

1.24.5 Expressing hunger and thirst

avoir faim/soif = *to be hungry/thirsty*

J'ai faim. — I am hungry.
As-tu faim? — Are you hungry?

Il a soif.	He is thirsty.
Nous avons soif.	We are thirsty.
Avez-vous faim?	Are you hungry?
Ils ont faim.	They are hungry.

1.24.6 Being right or wrong

avoir raison/tort = *to be right/wrong*

J'ai raison.	I am right.
Tu as raison!	You are right!
Il a tort.	He is wrong.
Nous avons raison.	We are right.
Vous avez tort!	You are wrong!
Ils ont tort.	They are wrong.

I How would you say the following?

a. We are right.
b. You are wrong.
c. I am hot.
d. He is thirsty.
e. They are hungry.
f. We are cold.
g. I am thirsty.
h. I need a beer.
i. We need a new car.
j. I am right.
k. They are wrong.
l. I am very cold.
m. They are hot.
n. We are thirsty.
o. I am afraid of spiders.
p. Are you thirsty?
q. Are you cold?
r. Are you hot?
s. Are you hungry?
t. Are you right?
u. You are wrong!
v. Are you afraid?
w. I am not afraid.
x. He is not afraid.
y. We are not afraid.
z. He is right.

1.24.7 Talking about not feeling well

Avoir is also used when talking about what is wrong with you: **avoir mal** = *to hurt*.

J'ai mal à la tête.	I have a headache.
As-tu mal à la jambe?	Does your leg hurt?
Il a mal aux dents.	He has toothache.
Nous avons mal aux pieds.	We have sore feet.
Avez-vous mal à la tête?	Have you got a headache?
Ils ont mal au cœur.	They feel sick.

Parts of the body which might hurt!

singular	plural	meaning
un œil	les yeux	eye(s)
une oreille	les oreilles	ear(s)
le dent	les dents	tooth/teeth
la main	les mains	hand(s)
le doigt	les doigts	finger(s)
le bras	les bras	arm(s)
la jambe	les jambes	leg(s)
le pied	les pieds	foot/feet
le dos		back

Le cœur (*heart*) is used to refer to *stomach ache/heartburn*.

II How would you say the following?

a. I have a headache.
b. Have you got toothache?
c. Her foot hurts.
d. My arms ache.
e. His knee hurts.
f. Have you got a headache?
g. She has earache.
h. Do you feel sick?
i. Does your back hurt?
j. He has backache.

1.25 Other problematic verbs

1.25.1 *se souvenir de* – to remember

In French, you remind yourself *of* something.

Je me souviens du moment où j'ai eu l'accident. — I remember the moment when I had the accident.
Je m'en souviens. — I remember it.
Je ne m'en souviens pas. — I don't remember it.

1.25.2 *savoir* and *connaître* – to know

Savoir is to know how to do something (as a result of learning how to do it).

Je sais conduire. — I know how to drive a car.
Je savais cuisiner. — I used to know how to cook.

Connaître is to know a person, thing or place (to recognise by seeing, hearing, tasting or touching).

Je le connais. — I know it/him.
Je l'ai connu. — I knew him.

1.25.3 to take and to bring

These English verbs can be translated in various ways.

- *prendre* – to take transport
  Je prends le bus. — I am taking the bus.
- *emporter* – to take away (something you can carry)
  une pizza à emporter — a take-away pizza
- *emmener* – to take (someone somewhere)
  J'ai emmené ma tante à l'aéroport. — I took my aunt to the airport.
- *apporter* – to bring (something you can carry)
  Je vous ai apporté un gâteau. — I have brought you a cake.
- *amener* – to bring (someone somewhere)
  Amenez un ami à la fête ce soir, si vous voulez. — Bring a guest to the party tonight, if you like.

Nouns

2.1 Recognising nouns

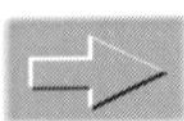

If you know what a noun is, go on to 2.2.

Nouns are naming words. They tell you who somebody is (e.g. *he is a soldier*, *she is a mother*) or what something is (e.g. *it is a table*, *it is a rainbow*).

You can recognise nouns because you can say 'the' or 'a' in front of them, e.g. a pencil, the dog, the house, the postman.

2.2 Gender of nouns and the definite article

The word *the* is called the definite article because it refers to a definite thing, e.g. the pen (which you are using) and not just any pen.

2.2.1 *Le* and *la*

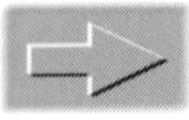

If you know about *le* ***and*** *la* ***and the gender of nouns, go on to 2.3.***

In French, all nouns are either masculine or feminine.

- The word for *the* in front of masculine nouns is *le*.

le garçon	the boy
le journal	the newspaper

- The word for *the* in front of feminine nouns is *la*.

la fille	the girl
la porte	the door

It is not always so easy to tell which words are going to be masculine or feminine. When you look a word up in the dictionary, it usually tells you the gender of the word in brackets after it: **maison** (f) *house* **appartement** (m) *flat*

I Put the correct form (le **or** la) **in front of these.**

a. ...... voiture (f) car
b. ...... valise (f) suitcase
c. ...... sac (m) bag
d. ...... portable (m) laptop or mobile phone
e. ...... calculette (f) calculator
f. ...... fichier (m) file
g. ...... carte bancaire (f) bank card
h. ...... réservation (f) reservation
i. ...... manteau (m) coat
j. ...... billet (m) ticket (for train/plane/ferry/theatre, etc.)
k. ...... ticket (m) ticket (for bus/cinema)

II Now do the same for these places.

a. ...... maison (f) house
b. ...... station-service (f) petrol station
c. ...... gare (m) station
d. ...... rue (f) street
e. ...... boulevard (m) avenue
f. ...... station de métro (f) underground station
g. ...... magasin (m) shop
h. ...... banque (f) bank
i. ...... poste (f) post office
j. ...... pont (m) bridge

2.2.2 L'

If the word begins with a vowel or silent **h**, you use **l'** for both masculine and feminine words as it makes them easier to say.

hôtel (m) l'hôtel hotel
avenue (f) l'avenue avenue

III Fill in the gaps with le, la **or** l'.

a. ...... appartement (m) flat
b. ...... château (m) castle
c. ...... école (f) school
d. ...... hôpital (m) hospital
e. ...... église (f) church
f. ...... mairie (m) town hall
g. ...... immeuble (m) block of flats

h.	...... hôtel (m)	hotel
i.	...... avenue (f)	avenue
j.	...... entrée (f)	entrance
k.	...... arbre (m)	tree
l.	...... bébé (m)	baby
m.	...... eau (f)	water
n.	...... enfant (m)	child
o.	...... homme (m)	man
p.	...... horloge (m)	clock
q.	...... rivière (f)	river
r.	...... rue (f)	street
s.	...... ville (f)	town
t.	...... village (m)	village

2.2.3 Shortcuts: masculine and feminine nouns

As it is not always possible to tell whether a word is masculine or feminine in French, it is helpful to learn the **le** or **la** when you learn it. However there are a few groups of words which are all masculine or all feminine.

These ones are all masculine:

- Words for male relations and jobs: *le père* (the father), *le garçon* (the boy), *le boulanger* (the baker).
- Days, months, seasons, weights and measures and languages: *le deux* (the number two), *le mercredi* (Wednesday), *l'hiver* (the winter), *le kilo* (the kilo), *le français* (the French language).
- Most words which have been adopted from English: *le short* (the shorts), *le jean* (the jeans), *le walkman* (the walkman), *le blues* (the blues), *le parking* (the car park).
- Countries, rivers, vegetables and fruit not ending in -e: *le Japon* (Japan), *le chou* (the cabbage), *le citron* (the lemon).
- Nouns which end in *-c: le lac* (the lake), *-é: le passé* (the past), *-eau**: *le bateau* (the boat) or *-ou: le trou* (the hole)

The exception to this is **l'eau** (*water*), which is feminine.

These words are all feminine:

- Female relations and female occupations: *la mère* (the mother), *la tante* (the aunt), *la boulangère* (the baker (f)).
- Most countries, rivers, vegetables and fruits ending in -e: *La Russie* (Russia), *La Seine* (the Seine), *la carotte* (the carrot), *la poire* (the pear). Exceptions: *le Rhône* (the Rhone), *le pamplemousse* (grapefruit).
- Shops: *la boutique* (the shop), *la boulangerie* (the baker's).

IV Using the above rules to help you, put the correct form of le **or** la **in front of these words.**

a. ...... dimanche
b. ...... salade
c. ...... Canada
d. ...... Loire
e. ...... gâteau
f. ...... printemps
g. ...... litre
h. ...... basket-ball
i. ...... tennis
j. ...... ski
k. ...... boucherie
l. ...... lundi
m. ...... pâtisserie
n. ...... France
o. ...... hockey
p. ...... marché
q. ...... Dordogne
r. ...... sweat-shirt
s. ...... château
t. ...... français

2.2.4 The plural

In the plural, the word for *the* becomes **les** for ALL nouns.

singular	**plural**
la maison le studio l'appartement	les maisons les studios les appartements

To make the plural of the noun in English, we usually add an **-s**. In French, most words make their plural in the same way, by adding **-s**.

la maison → les maisons; le chien → les chiens; la rue → les rues

The ***-s*** *is not pronounced when saying the word, so the singular and plural sound the same.*

2.2.5 Common irregular plurals

The following categories form their plurals in different ways.

- Most words which end in *-al* form their plural in *-aux* (pronounced 'o').
  un journal – a newspaper → deux journaux – two newspapers
  un cheval – a horse → deux chevaux – two horses
  un animal – an animal → trois animaux – three animals
- Most words which end in *-au*, *-eau* and *-eu* add *-x*.
  un manteau – a coat → cinq manteaux – five coats
  un neveu – a nephew → trois neveux – three nephews
  BUT
  le pneu – the tyre → les pneus – the tyres

- Seven words ending in *-ou* and *-x*: *genou* – knee, *caillou* – pebble, *bijou* – jewel, *joujou* – toy, *hibou* – owl, *chou* – cabbage, *pou* – louse.
  un genou → deux genoux
- Other words ending in *-ou* form their plural with *-s*.
  le trou – the hole → les trous – the holes
- Two words which are mostly used in the plural are *un cheveu* – a (single) hair → *les cheveux* – hair and *un œil* – an eye → *les yeux* – the eyes.
- Words which already end in *-s*, *-x*, or *-z* don't change in the plural.
  le bras – the arm → les bras – the arms
  le prix – the price → les prix – the prices
  le nez – the nose → les nez – the noses

V Put these words into the plural.

a.	l'animal	the animal
b.	l'oiseau	the bird
c.	le genou	the knee
d.	le cheval	the horse
e.	le bateau	the boat
f.	le journal	the newspaper
g.	le château	the castle
h.	le neveu	the nephew
i.	le cadeau	the present

VI Write out the plural forms of these words. Check what they already end in first!

a.	le fils	the son
b.	le Français	the Frenchman
c.	l'Anglais	the Englishman
d.	la croix	the cross
e.	le repas	the meal
f.	le feu	the fire
g.	le pneu	the tyre
h.	le chou	the cabbage
i.	le bois	the wood
j.	la souris	the mouse

2.3 Nouns and the indefinite article

The word *a* is called the indefinite article because it refers to any one item and not a specific one: a bottle of red wine, not *the* bottle that you have chosen specifically.

- The word for *a* in front of masculine noun is *un*.
  un verre — a glass
- The word for *a* in front of feminine noun is *une*.
  une bouteille — a bottle

I Imagine this is your family. How would you say you have one of all these?

J'ai . . .

a.	. . . . . . frère	**f.**	. . . . . . tante
b.	. . . . . . sœur	**g.**	. . . . . . beau-père
c.	. . . . . . grand-père	**h.**	. . . . . . cousine
d.	. . . . . . grand-mère	**i.**	. . . . . . belle-mère
e.	. . . . . . oncle	**j.**	. . . . . . chien

In French, you omit the indefinite article when talking about jobs or professions.

Il est étudiant. — He is a student.
Elle est vétérinaire. — She is a vet.
M. Brown est médecin. — Mr Brown is a doctor.
Mme Gibbs est professeur de dessin. — Mrs Gibbs is an art teacher.

2.4 Partitive articles: *some, any*

The partitive article is the grammatical name for the words which translate *some* or *any*. It refers to an unspecified quantity, e.g. **le sucre** (*the sugar*) → **du sucre** (*some/any sugar*).

2.4.1 *Du, de la, de l'* or *des?*

The partitive article in French is made up of **de** (*of*) and the definite article (**le**, **la**, **l'** or **les**).

> ***De** + **le** becomes **du** and **de** + **les** becomes **des**.*
> ***De l'** is used before both masculine and feminine nouns which begin with a vowel or a silent **h**.*

masculine	**feminine**	**plural**
du (de l')	de la (de l')	des

Je voudrais du pain. — I would like some bread.
Avez-vous du pain? — Have you got any bread?

I How would you ask for some of these?

Avez-vous . . . ?

a. . . . . . . sucre (m)
b. . . . . . . huile (f)
c. . . . . . . beurre (m)
d. . . . . . . pain de campagne (m)
e. . . . . . . petits pains (pl)
f. . . . . . . cognac (m)
g. . . . . . . lait (m)
h. . . . . . . pommes (pl)
i. . . . . . . confiture (f)
j. . . . . . . miel (m)

In English, we sometimes miss out the word *some* or *any*, but in French you must put it in.

II Que buvez-vous? **Put in the correct form:** du, de la **or** de l'.

Je bois . . . I drink

a. . . . . . . bière (f)
b. . . . . . . vin (m)
c. . . . . . . limonade (f)
d. . . . . . . coca-cola (m)
e. . . . . . . lait (m)
f. . . . . . . café (m)
g. . . . . . . thé (m)
h. . . . . . . jus d'orange (m)
i. . . . . . . eau (f)
j. . . . . . . champagne (m)

III Add the correct form of un/une **or** des.

Je porte . . . I am wearing

a.	. . . . . . manteau noir.	a black coat
b.	. . . . . . chapeau de fourrure.	a fur hat
c.	. . . . . . gants en cuir.	leather gloves
d.	. . . . . . écharpe en soie rouge.	a red silk scarf
e.	. . . . . . chemise blanche.	a white shirt
f.	. . . . . . costume gris.	a grey suit
g.	. . . . . . chaussettes grises.	grey socks
h.	. . . . . . chaussures noires.	black shoes
i.	. . . . . . parapluie noir.	a black umbrella
j.	. . . . . . journal sous le bras.	a newspaper under my arm

2.4.2 How to say 'not any'

When *any* follows a negative statement (e.g. *I don't have any/I don't drink any*), you use **de** for both masculine and feminine words. You always need to use **de** in French, even when you drop the *any* in English.

Je ne veux pas de café.	I don't want any coffee.
Je ne mange pas de salade.	I don't eat salad.

***De** changes to **d'** before a vowel or a silent **h**.*

IV Say what is not available. Use Il n'y a pas . . . **(There isn't any . . .).**

a. ketchup
b. confiture
c. mayonnaise
d. sucre
e. lait
f. beurre
g. fromage
h. soupe
i. jus d'orange
j. yaourt

V Now say that you don't eat these things. Use je ne mange pas . . .

a. noix (pl) – walnuts
b. cacahuètes (pl) – peanuts
c. sucreries (pl) – sweets
d. viande (f) – meat
e. poisson (m) – fish
f. laitue (f) – lettuce
g. tomates (pl) – tomatoes
h. légumes (pl) – vegetables
i. pain (m) – bread
j. escargots (pl) – snails

2.4.3 Other expressions with *de* or *d'*

The following expressions are very common, so it's worth learning them.

J'ai beaucoup de	I have a lot of
J'ai assez de	I have enough (of)
J'ai trop de	I have too much/many (of)

Try saying them aloud to get used to the sound of them.

VI How would you say you have lots of the following?

a. livres
b. BDs
c. CDs
d. photos

VII Now say that you have enough of the following.

a. essence
b. argent
c. informations
d. temps
e. catalogues

VIII Finally, say that you have too much/many of the following.

a. travail
b. invitations
c. déplacements
d. bagages
e. papiers

2.5 *À* and the definite article

When **à** is used in front of the definite article, it changes in the masculine and plural.

- *à + le* becomes *au*
- *à + les* becomes *aux*
- before words beginning with a vowel or silent *h*, you use *à l'*

masculine	feminine	plural
au (à l')	à la (à l')	aux

2.5.1 *À* + article used in answer to the question, 'What kind of?'

Quelle sorte de sandwich/glace?	What kind of sandwich/ice cream?
Un sandwich au fromage./Une glace au chocolat.	A cheese sandwich./A chocolate ice cream.

I Quel parfum? **Say what sort of ice cream you would like.**

Je voudrais une glace . . .

a. . . . . . . la vanille
b. . . . . . . le citron
c. . . . . . . la pistache
d. . . . . . . le cassis
e. . . . . . . l'abricot
f. . . . . . . le chocolat
g. . . . . . . la banane
h. . . . . . . la fraise
i. . . . . . . l'orange
j. . . . . . . la mangue

II Now say what sort of sandwich you would like.

Je voudrais un sandwich . . .

a. . . . . . . le jambon
b. . . . . . . le poulet

c. ...... le saucisson
d. ...... le fromage
e. ...... la sardine
f. ...... le thon
g. ...... les rillettes
h. ...... le camembert

Remember that the final ***-x*** *in* ***aux*** *is not pronounced . . .*
une tarte aux fraises, une glace aux fruits rouges, une omelette aux fines herbes
. . . unless it is followed by a word beginning with a vowel, and then it sounds like an 's' at the beginning of the next word.
un flan aux‿asperges, une quiche aux‿épinards, un gâteau aux‿amandes

2.5.2 *À* + article used to translate 'at the' or 'to the'

Je vais au bureau.	I am going to the office.

III Say where you are going.

Je vais . . .
a. ...... la plage
b. ...... l'hôtel
c. ...... la piscine
d. ...... l'hôpital
e. ...... le musée
f. ...... le cinéma
g. ...... le théâtre
h. ...... la station-service
i. ...... la banque
j. ...... la gare

IV How would you ask the way to these places in Rouen?

Excusez-moi, pourriez-vous m'indiquer comment aller . . . ?
a. ...... l'église St-Ouen
b. ...... la cathédrale Jeanne d'Arc
c. ...... le Gros Horloge
d. ...... l'Hôtel de Ville
e. ...... la rue des Capucines
f. ...... le musée du Théâtre
g. ...... l'office du tourisme
h. ...... la Seine
i. ...... la Place du marché
j. ...... les toilettes publiques

Pronouns

A pronoun is a word which stands for a noun so that instead of saying *Mr Jones*, you can say *he*, instead of saying *the lady*, you can say *she*, and instead of *my husband/wife and I*, you can say *we*.

3.1 Subject pronouns

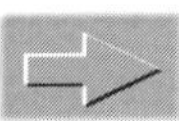

If you know what a subject pronoun is go on to 3.2.

The subject is the person or thing who does the action.

I run, *you* play, *he* eats, *she* drinks, *it* shuts, *we* live, *you* swim, *they* talk

The subject pronouns in French are as follows.

	singular	**plural**
first person **second person** **third person**	je – I tu – you il – he/it elle – she/it on – one	nous – we vous – you ils – they elles – they

3.1.1 First person

Je *in front of a word beginning with a vowel becomes* **j'**. It is only written with a capital letter at the beginning of a sentence.

3.1.2 Second person

There are two forms of the word for *you*, **tu** and **vous**.

- **Tu** is used in the singular and only when talking to someone you know well who has invited you to do so, or to a child.

- **Vous** is often referred to as the 'polite' form, as it is used not only in the plural but also when talking to someone older than you or to a stranger, even if there is only one person.

There is a special verb which means *to call someone tu* – **tutoyer** – and a verb which means *to call someone vous* – **vouvoyer**.

3.1.3 Third person

Remember that everything in French is either masculine or feminine. *A chair* is feminine, so if you want to say anything about *it*, you have to use **elle** (*she*); similarly, *a book* is masculine so if you want to refer to *it*, you have to say **il** (*he*).

In the plural, you use **ils** to refer to more than one masculine person or thing, or to a mixture of masculine and feminine things. You only use **elles** if all the people or things are feminine words, so if you have a group of ten ladies and one man, you must still refer to them as **ils**.

I Which pronoun would you use in these sentences?

a. Jean habite en France. ......habite dans le Nord.
b. Paul et Marianne habitent dans le Sud. ...... habitent à Marseille.
c. Moi? ......habite à Paris.
d. Où habitez-...... ?
e. J'habite à Paris avec mes amis. ......habitons un grand immeuble boulevard Haussmann.
f. Séverine et Emmanuelle habitent dans la banlieue nord. ...... ont un petit appartement.
g. Ma sœur habite à Lyon. ...... fait ses études à l'université Lyon III.
h. Mes grands-parents habitent en Auvergne. ......ont une ferme.
i. Où habites-...... ?
j. Mon frère joue au tennis. ...... joue très bien.

3.2 Direct object pronouns

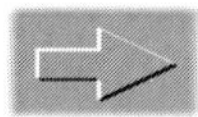

If you know what a direct object pronoun is and how to use it, go on to 3.3.

The direct object is the person or thing who has the action done to it.

John called *me*, he saw *you*, they bought *it*, they found *her*, Elisabeth saw *us*, we saw *you*, we know *them*

I Which are the direct object pronouns in these English sentences?

a. He sees me.
b. I see him.

c. They see us.
d. We see them.
e. I see you.
f. I am eating them.
g. She is making it.
h. He finds them.
i. They find us.
j. We find you.

In English, direct objects come after the verb.

3.2.1 French direct object pronouns

	singular	**plural**
first person	me – me	nous – us
second person	te – you	vous – you
third person	le – him/it la – her/it	les – them

In French, they come in front of the verb.

Je le/la/les vois.	I see him/her/them.
Il me/nous voit.	He sees me/us.
Ils te/vous voient.	They see you.

*When you don't know whether the person or thing is masculine or feminine, use **le**.*

II Put the correct pronoun in these sentences.

a.	He sees me.	Il . . . . . . voit.
b.	I see him.	Je . . . . . . vois.
c.	I eat them.	Je . . . . . . mange.
d.	I don't eat it (meat).	Je ne . . . . . . mange pas.
e.	The children don't watch them (films).	Les enfants ne . . . . . . regardent pas.
f.	I am making it (the cake).	Je . . . . . . fais.
g.	She is eating it (the biscuit).	Elle . . . . . . mange.
h.	Mr Durand is buying them (cigars).	M. Durand . . . . . . achète.
i.	Mrs Durand does not smoke them.	Mme Durand ne . . . . . . fume pas.
j.	Mr Pernod doesn't like you.	M. Pernod ne . . . . . . aime pas.
k.	They saw us.	Ils . . . . . . ont vus.
l.	We saw them.	Nous . . . . . . avons vus.
m.	He bought it (the car).	Il . . . . . . a achetée.
n.	They found you.	Ils . . . . . . ont trouvés.
o.	He pushed me.	Il . . . . . . a poussé(e).

p.	I missed it (the bus).	Je . . . . . .ai raté.
q.	We ate them.	Nous . . . . . . avons mangés.
r.	Have you lost it (the cat)?	Vous . . . . . .avez perdu?
s.	My husband saw it (the cat).	Mon mari . . . . . .a vu.
t.	We will find it (the cat).	Nous . . . . . . trouverons.

3.2.2 Past participle agreement

You only need this for written French. It does not alter the pronunciation.

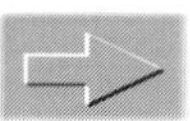

If you are not going to need it, go on to 3.3.

In the perfect tense, the past participle 'agrees' with a direct object if the direct object comes in front of the verb. 'Agreement' means adding the following endings to the past participle.

singular		**plural**	
masculine	**feminine**	**masculine**	**feminine**
–	-e	-s	-es

Je l'ai vu.	I saw him.
Je l'ai vue.	I saw her.
Je les ai achetés.	I bought them (the onions).
Je les ai achetées.	I bought them (the apples).

The past participle also agrees with the object if the object comes in front of the subject and the relative pronoun **que**.

Le temps qu'il a perdu . . .	The time that he has lost . . .
La maison que j'ai vue . . .	The house that I have seen . . .
Les courses qu'elle a faites . . .	The shopping that she did . . .
Les verres qu'il a cassé . . .	The glasses that he broke . . .

III Replace the word in italics with le, la **or** les.

Martin a vu *son amie* – Il l'a vue

a. Il a vu *son ami.*
b. Il a vu *ses amis.*
c. Il a vu *ses amies.*
d. Il a perdu *sa montre.*
e. Il a acheté *la nouvelle montre.*
f. Il a trouvé *sa montre.*
g. Il a donné *la nouvelle montre* à son amie.

IV Add an ending to the past participle, where necessary.

Jean-Claude . . .

a. La femme qu'il a aimé.
b. Le livres qu'il a lu.
c. Les émissions qu'il a regardé.
d. La voiture qu'il a conduit.
e. Les papiers qu'il a signé.
f. Les mensonges qu'il a dit.
g. Son ami qu'il a trahi.

3.3 Indirect object pronouns

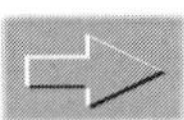

If you know what an indirect object pronoun is and how to use it, go on to 3.4.

In English, an indirect object pronoun is the same as a direct object pronoun but has (or can have) *to* or *for* in front of it.

I bought her it. = I bought it (direct object – it is the thing that you bought) for her (indirect object).
Give me it. = Give it (direct object) to me (indirect object).
They showed him it. = They showed it (direct object) to him (indirect object).

I Identify the indirect object pronouns in these English sentences.

a. He lent me his pen.
b. I wrote them a letter.
c. He read it to them.
d. They sent me a reply.
e. I gave it to him.
f. He translated it for me.
g. He wrote them an explanation.
h. I bought her some chocolates.
i. I told them I would be late.
j. I gave him a new pen for his help.

3.3.1 French indirect object pronouns

	singular	**plural**
first person	me – to me	nous – to us
second person	te – to you	vous – to you
third person	lui – to him/her/it	leur – to them

In French, you always put the indirect object pronoun in front of the verb.

Il me donne des fleurs.	He gives (to) me flowers.
Je vous donne un coup de fil.	I'll give you a call.
Je lui envoie un fax.	I am sending him/her a fax.
Nous leur avons donné les billets.	We have given them the tickets.
Vous ne nous avez pas donné les clés.	You haven't given us the keys.

II Fill in the missing pronouns.

a. Il . . . . . . prête son stylo. (her)
b. Je . . . . . . envoie une lettre. (them)
c. Il . . . . . . raconte une histoire. (me)
d. Nous . . . . . . achetons un cadeau. (them)
e. Vous . . . . . . donnez une invitation. (us)
f. M. Bertrand . . . . . . présente sa femme. (you)
g. Nous . . . . . . offrons des fleurs. (her)
h. Elle . . . . . . remercie. (us)
i. Je . . . . . . dis 'Bon anniversaire!' (him)
j. On . . . . . . offre une bouteille de cognac. (them)

3.4 Other pronouns: *y*

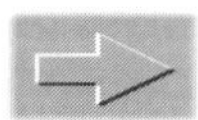

If you know about* y*, go on to 3.5.

Y -*there* stands for a place that you have already mentioned. It always goes in front of the verb.

John est allé en Grèce.	John has been to Greece.
Il y est allé deux fois.	He has been (there) twice.
Y êtes-vous déjà allé?	Have you been (there)?

Sometimes we would miss it out in English, but you need to put it in in French.

Il va en ville.	He is going to town.
J'y vais aussi.	I am going (there) too.
Allons-y!	Let's go (there).

Try reading them aloud to get used to the sound of the sentence.

I In the following sentences, replace the name of the place (shown in italics) with the pronoun y**. For example:**

Bénédicte va à Paris. → Bénédicte y va.

a. Monique habite *à Lyon*.
b. Je vais *en ville*.
c. Nous allons *au cinéma* au moins trois fois par mois.
d. Êtes-vous jamais allés *en Ecosse*?

e. Ils mangent souvent *au restaurant.*
f. Oh! Il faisait beau *sur la côte d'Azur.*
g. Nous avons fait de la planche à voile *sur le lac d'Annecy.*
h. Il a écouté le Requiem de Mozart *à la phonotèque.*
i. Nous achetons nos fruits et nos légumes *au marché.*
j. Manges-tu souvent *au McDo*?

Y is also used to translate: *in it/them*, *about it/them*, etc.

Je ne m'y intéresse pas.	I am not interested (in it/them).
Je n'y pense jamais.	I don't ever think about it/them.

3.5 Other pronouns: *en*

En refers to something you have already mentioned and stands for *of it* or *of them*.

J'en ai beaucoup.	I've got a lot (of them).
Les escargots? J'en mange.	I eat (some of) them.
Je n'en mange pas.	I don't eat them.

Like **y**, we often miss it out in English, but you must include it in French.

Les photos de Liam? En avez-vous?	The photos of Liam? Have you any (of them)?
J'en ai beaucoup.	I've got a lot (of them).
Je n'en ai pas.	I haven't any (of them).

I Rephrase these sentences using en **instead of the word in italics. Remember to put** en **in front of the verb!**

a. J'ai beaucoup *de CDs.*
b. Il n'a pas *d'ordinateur.*
c. Il a trois *stylos.*
d. Combien *de livres* avez-vous?
e. Nous avons beaucoup de différents *vins.*
f. Avez-vous *des cigarettes*?
g. Ils ont trois *chiens.*
h. Avez-vous une *voiture*?
i. Oui, j'ai une *nouvelle voiture.*
j. Mon ami n'a pas *de voiture.*

If you need to replace ***à*** *+ noun, use* ***y****. If you need to replace* ***de*** *+ noun, use* ***en****.*

3.5.1 *Devoir, pouvoir, savoir, vouloir* and *falloir*

These verbs are usually used together with another verb, and the pronoun comes in front of the verb it refers to (which will be the second verb or the infinitive).

Je dois les surveiller.	I have to keep an eye on them.
Il ne peut pas y aller.	He can't go there.
Vous savez le faire.	You know how to do it.
Elle veut en avoir.	She wants to have some.
Il faut le finir.	We/You have to finish it.

II Replace the words in italics with a pronoun.

a. Nous ne pouvons pas aller *à Paris.*
b. Je dois payer *l'addition.*
c. Vous savez comment utiliser *le fax.*
d. Elle veut acheter *une carte* pour la fête des mères.
e. Il faut aller *à la poste.*
f. Il peut lire *le journal* maintenant.

3.6 Word order of pronouns

If you have more than one pronoun in front of the verb, they always go in the following order.

je tu il/elle/on nous vous ils/elles	(ne)	me te se nous vous	le la les les	lui leur	y	en	**verb**	(pas)

*Remember **en** always goes at the end.*

I How would you say the following?

a. He saw me.
b. She saw him.
c. He bought it (the car).
d. She didn't like him.
e. I can do it.
f. I can't do it.

g. We went there.
h. They accompanied us.
i. I bought some.
j. I threw them away. (les journaux)

II How would you say the following?
a. He gave it to me. (son numéro de téléphone)
b. I gave it to her.
c. She gave it to them.
d. They gave it to you.
e. You gave it to us.
f. She bought him it. (le livre)
g. He read it.
h. He gave it to us.
i. We gave it to you.
j. They read it to them.

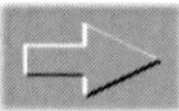

If you have had enough pronouns move on to 4 Adjectives and come back later.

3.7 Emphatic pronouns

These are used for emphasis and are only used when talking about people or animals.

Qui est là? Moi!	Who is there? Me!
A-t-il une voiture? Lui? Non!	Has he got a car? What, him? No!

Emphatic pronouns are also used after prepositions: **avec moi** (*with me*), **sans lui** (*without him*), **pour eux** (*for them*), **selon moi** (*in my opinion*), **chez toi** (*at your house*), etc.

C'est à moi.	It's mine.
Il est avec moi.	He's with me.
Nous achetons un cadeau pour elle.	We're buying a present for her.
Il est parti sans elle.	He went without her.

They are also used with the imperative (for people).

Attendez-moi!	Wait for me!

3.7.1 French emphatic pronouns

	singular	plural
first person	moi me	nous us
second person	toi you	vous you
third person	lui him	eux them, (m)
	elle her	elles them, (f)

I Replace the people in italics with the right form of the emphatic pronoun.

a. Ce stylo est à *Jean-Pierre*.
b. Maurice est allé en ville sans *sa femme*.
c. Elle est sortie avec *ses amies*.
d. M. Bertrand a acheté un cadeau pour *sa fille*.
e. Le sac bleu est à *Sylvain*, et le sac rouge est à *Maurice*.
f. As-tu vu le film, *Maurice*?
g. Il a mangé avec *moi et mes enfants*.
h. Nous sommes partis sans *nos enfants*.
i. On a acheté des glaces pour *toi et tes copains*.
j. C'est *Marc*!

II How would you say the following?

a.	Are you coming with me?	Vous venez avec ...... ?
b.	I am going with him.	Je vais avec ....
c.	He went without us.	Il est parti sans ....
d.	We will leave without her.	Nous partirons sans ....
e.	We are buying it for you.	Nous l'achetons pour ....
f.	In his opinion, we are too old.	Selon ...... nous sommes trop vieux.
g.	In my opinion, he is wrong.	Selon ...... il a tort.
h.	We are going without him.	Nous allons sans ....
i.	They are going without her.	Ils vont sans ....
j.	She is coming with us.	Elle vient avec ....

3.8 Order of pronouns in the imperative

The pronouns come after the verb and are hyphenated to it.

This is easy to remember, as the order is just the same as it is in English!

Regardez-moi.	Look at me.
Tenez-le.	Hold it.
Choisissez-le.	Choose it.
Donne-le-moi.	Give it to me.
Restez-y.	Stay there.
Achetez-en.	Buy some.
Mangez-les.	Eat them.

The pronouns used in the imperative are as follows.

le la les	moi toi lui nous vous leur	en y

3.9 Interrogative pronouns

An interrogative pronoun is used to ask the question *Who?* or *What?*. In French. You use **qui?** (*who?*) when talking about a person and **que?** (*what?*) when talking about a thing.

You can use the short form . . .

Qui?	Who?
Qui dit ça?	Who says that?
Que?	What?
Que dit-il?	What is he saying?

. . . or the long form.

Qui est-ce qui . . . ?	Who (is it that) . . . ?
Qui est-ce qui dit ça?	Who (is it that) says that?
Qu'est-ce que . . . ?	What (is it that) . . . ?
Qu'est-ce qu'il dit?	What is (it that) he (is) saying?

Note that with the short form, you have to invert the subject and the verb. With the long form, the word order stays the same.

3.9.1 *Qui* or *que?*

If the word comes in front of the verb, it will be the subject, and if it comes after it, it will be the object.

I Ask about the person or thing in italics. What question would you ask? For example:

Michel arrive en premier. → Qui arrive/Qui est-ce qui arrive en premier?

a. Jean-Luc porte *un pantalon rouge et un pull bleu.*

b. *Thomas* joue au basket.

c. Nous mangeons *du pain grillé.*

d. Jérôme fait *sa déclaration d'impôts.*

e. Je veux *un billet aller retour.*

f. Vous buvez *de l'eau.*

g. *Elvire* va au cinéma.

3.10 Possessive pronouns

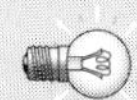

You can avoid using possessive pronouns by using the expression ***c'est à*** *... and the emphatic pronouns (see 3.7 above).*

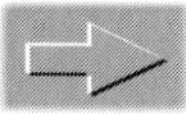

If you prefer to avoid the possessive pronouns, go on to 3.11.

Possessive pronouns translate the English *mine*, *yours*, *his*, *hers*, *ours*, *yours*, *theirs*. They have to agree with the noun they are replacing.

	singular		**plural**	
	masculine	**feminine**	**masculine**	**feminine**
mine	le mien	la mienne	les miens	les miennes
yours	le tien	la tienne	les tiens	les tiennes
his/hers/its	le sien	la sienne	les siens	les siennes
ours	le nôtre	la nôtre	les nôtres	les nôtres
yours	le vôtre	la vôtre	les vôtres	les vôtres
theirs	le leur	la leur	les leurs	les leurs

Regardez cette voiture, c'est la mienne. (la mienne to agree with voiture)	Look at this car, it's mine.
C'est à moi.	It's mine.
Ce porte-monnaie, c'est le sien. (le sien to agree with porte-monnaie)	This purse is hers.
C'est à elle.	It's hers.

I Replace the nouns in italics with the correct form of the pronoun.

a. *Ce stylo* est à moi. C'est *le mien.*
b. *Ces stylos* sont à moi. Ce sont ....
c. *Cette voiture* est à mon père. C'est ....
d. *Ces livres* sont à ma grand-mère. Ce sont ....
e. *Cette tasse* est à vous. C'est ....
f. *Ces revues* sont à mes frères. Ce sont ....
g. *Cette moto* est à vous? C'est ...... ?
h. *Ces frites* sont pour nous. Ce sont ....
i. *Ces glaces* sont pour vous. Ce sont ....

3.11 Relative pronouns

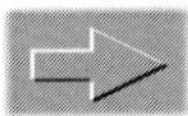

If you can recognise a relative pronoun, go on to 3.12.

Relative pronouns are the words *who*, *which* and *whose* when they are used to refer to someone already mentioned.

la femme *qui* habite à côté	The lady *who* lives next door
le chien *qui* aboie toute la nuit	the dog *which* barks all night
mon portable *qui* ne marche plus	my mobile *which* doesn't work any more
le livre *que* nous venons d'acheter	the book *which* we have just bought
l'homme *dont* la voiture est toujours garée devant notre maison	the man *whose* car is always parked in front of our house

The part of the sentence after the relative pronoun is called a relative clause.

A 'clause' is the name for subordinate or lesser part of a sentence which doesn't make sense on its own but needs the rest of the sentence to make it make sense.

3.11.1 Relative pronouns *qui, que, dont*

Qui – who/which

Qui always refers to the subject of the sentence. In the following clause, **qui** is the subject of the verb **porte**.

la femme qui porte une robe bleue — the woman who wears a blue dress

Que – whom/which

Que refers to the object of the sentence. In the following clause, **que** is the object of **je vois**.

la femme que je vois — the woman (that) I see

Dont – whose/of whom/of which

la femme dont je connais le mari	the lady whose husband I know
la personne dont j'ai oublié le nom	the person whose name I have forgotten

I Which relative pronoun would you use?

a.	The man in the suit and tie is called Mr Bertrand.	L'homme ...... est venu en costume-cravate s'appelle M. Bertrand.
b.	The man I don't know is wearing the sunglasses.	L'homme ...... je ne connais pas porte des lunettes de soleil.
c.	The man whose wife is ill isn't coming.	L'homme ...... la femme est malade ne vient pas.
d.	The person I was waiting for didn't arrive.	La personne ...... j'attendais n'est pas arrivée.

e.	The person whose address you gave me isn't at that address any more.	La personne ...... vous m'avez donné l'adresse n'est plus à cet adresse.
f.	The person who wants to buy the flat has already put in an offer.	La personne ...... veut acheter l'immeuble a déjà fait une offre.

3.12 How to say *Which one?*

After a preposition **lequel** is used for things.

singular		plural	
masculine	**feminine**	**masculine**	**feminine**
lequel	laquelle	lesquels	lesquelles

Nous avons six chiots. Lequel voulez-vous?	We have six puppies. Which one would you like?
Regardez les maisons à louer. Laquelle préférez-vous?	Look at the houses to let. Which would you prefer?
Essayez nos nouveaux parfums. Lesquel aimez-vous?	Try our new perfumes. Which ones do you like?

3.13 Demonstrative pronouns

Demonstrative pronouns are so called because they point out a particular one.

3.13.1 The one which/whose/etc.

The pronouns agree with the noun they represent and are followed by **qui/que** or a preposition.

singular		plural	
masculine	**feminine**	**masculine**	**feminine**
celui	celle	ceux	celles

J'ai donné la photo à mon cousin, celle de ma tante le jour de son mariage.	I gave the photo to my cousin, the one of my aunt on her wedding day.

Avez-vous vu mon stylo, celui que mon père m'a donné pour mes 21 ans? — Have you seen my pen, the one my father gave me for my 21st?

Il faut changer les fleurs, celles dans le vase de la salle à manger. — You must change the flowers, the ones in the vase in the dining-room.

Achetez des haricots, ceux qui sont les plus beaux. — Buy some beans, the ones which are the nicest.

3.13.2 This one/that one

Celui-ci can also mean the former and **celui-là** the latter.

	singular		**plural**	
	masculine	**feminine**	**masculine**	**feminine**
this/these one(s) (here)	celui-ci	celle-ci	ceux-ci	celles-ci
that/those one(s) (there)	celui-là	celle-là	ceux-là	celles-là

Quelle bague préférez-vous? — Which ring do you prefer?
Je préfère celle-ci. — I prefer this one (here).
Vous préférez celle-là. — You prefer that one (there).

Quelle porte-monnaie préférez-vous? — Which purse do you prefer?
Je préfère celui-là. — I prefer that one (there).
Vous préférez celui-ci. — You prefer this one (here).

I Say you want to change these things.

Je voudrais changer . . .

a. these gloves — gant (m)
b. this ring — bague (f)
c. that purse — porte-monnaie (m)
d. those shoes — chaussure (f)
e. these lamps — lampe (f)
f. that tyre — pneu (m)
g. this pullover — pull (m)
h. those books — livre (m)

4

Adjectives

4.1 Adjectives and adjectival agreement

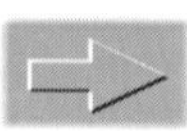

If you know what an adjective is, go on to 4.1.1.

Adjectives are 'describing' words; you use them to say what something or someone is like.

I Highlight the adjectives in these sentences.

a. Jack is tall and very sporty.
b. He has short, dark hair and blue-grey eyes.
c. He has a new, blue car.
d. He likes to wear smart clothes when he goes to work and casual clothes at the weekend.
e. His house is quite small but it has a big garden.
f. His girlfriend is small and bubbly.
g. She manages a large bank.
h. He has an older brother and a younger sister.
i. His favourite dish is tagliatelle alla carbonara.
j. He likes his coffee very hot and very black.

4.1.1 Adjectival agreement

In French the adjective 'agrees' with the noun.

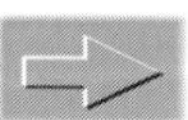

If you know about adjectival agreement, go on to 4.2.

- If the noun is feminine singular, most adjectives add *-e* (unless they already end in *-e*).
- If the noun is masculine plural, most adjectives add *-s*.
- If the noun is feminine plural, most adjectives add *-es*.

singular		**plural**	
masculine	**feminine**	**masculine**	**feminine**
– petit timide	-e petite timide	-s petits timides	-es petites timides

In French, most endings are not pronounced, so many adjectives sound the same in all forms BUT if the adjective ends in ***-d, -s*** *or* ***-t****, the added* ***-e*** *and* ***-es*** *will mean that you have to pronounce the final* ***-d/-s/-t****. So* ***grand*** *is pronounced gr-aa-n, but* ***grande*** *is pronounced gr-aa-nd; similarly* ***petit*** *= pe-ti and* ***petite*** *= pe-teet; and* ***gris*** *is pronounced gri, but* ***grise*** *sounds something like greaze.*

II Fill in the missing forms and then try saying them aloud and note which ones will sound different.

		singular		**plural**	
	meaning	**masculine**	**feminine**	**masculine**	**feminine**
a.	happy	content			
b.	sad	triste			
c.	short	court			
d.	tall/big	grand			
e.	weak	faible			
f.	strong	fort			
g.	intelligent	intelligent			
h.	stupid	stupide			
i.	pretty	joli			
j.	ugly	laid			
k.	fun	marrant			
l.	naughty	méchant			
m.	bad	mauvais			
n.	young	jeune			
o.	wide	large			
p.	thin	mince			
q.	modern	moderne			
r.	clean	propre			
s.	dirty	sale			
t.	friendly	aimable			

III Which form of the adjective in brackets would you use to complete these sentences?

a. John a les cheveux . . . . (court)
b. Il est . . . . (content)
c. Il a une . . . . . . sœur qui s'appelle Louise. (petit)
d. Et deux . . . . . . frères qui s'appellent Yann et Serge. (grand)
e. Louise est . . . . (joli)
f. Yann et Serge sont . . . . (mince)
g. Ils ont les cheveux . . . . (noir)
h. Louise est très . . . . (intelligent)
i. Mais elle est souvent . . . . (méchant)
j. Yann et Serge sont . . . . (marrant)
k. Patrice habite une . . . . . . ville. (petit)
l. Il habite un quartier . . . . (calme)
m. Le lôtissement où il habite est . . . . (moderne)
n. Les maisons sont assez . . . . (grand)
o. Il a un . . . . . . jardin. (petit)
p. Le salon est . . . . (grand)
q. La cuisine est assez . . . . (petit)
r. Et les chambres ne sont pas . . . . . . non plus. (grand)
s. Il a une . . . . . . vue de son bureau. (joli)
t. Il préfère les maisons . . . . (moderne)

4.1.2 Irregular adjectives

Adjectives which end in -f

These make the feminine by replacing the **-f** *with* **-ve**.

	singular		**plural**	
meaning	**masculine**	**feminine**	**masculine**	**feminine**
active sporty new	actif sportif neuf	active sportive neuve	actifs sportifs neufs	actives sportives neuves

Adjectives which end in -x

These make the feminine by replacing the **-x** with **-se**.

	singular		**plural**	
meaning	**masculine**	**feminine**	**masculine**	**feminine**
dreadful ambitious boring	affreux ambitieux ennuyeux	affreuse ambitieuse ennuyeuse	affreux ambitieux ennuyeux	affreuses ambitieuses ennuyeuses

meaning	singular		plural	
	masculine	**feminine**	**masculine**	**feminine**
generous happy joyful serious	généreux heureux joyeux sérieux	généreuse heureuse joyeuse sérieuse	généreux heureux joyeux sérieux	généreuses heureuses joyeuses sérieuses

Other adjectives which end in -x

meaning	singular		plural	
	masculine	**feminine**	**masculine**	**feminine**
old soft/sweet false/wrong	vieux (vieil*) doux faux	vieille douce fausse	vieux doux faux	vieilles douces fausses

* You use **vieil** before masculine nouns beginning with a vowel or silent **h**.

IV Choose the right form of the adjectives in brackets.

a. M. Barnard est très .... (actif)
b. Mme Barnard n'est pas .... (sportif)
c. Les filles Barnard sont .... (sportif)
d. Leurs fils, Etienne et Marc, sont .... (paresseux)
e. Mme Dubois n'est pas .... (vieux)
f. Son fils, Nicolas, est très .... (ambitieux)
g. Ses filles, Marianne et Laurence, ne sont pas .... (heureux)
h. Le film était .... (ennuyeux)
i. Les chiens sont .... (heureux)
j. Mon chat est .... (paresseux)
k. Marilène est .... (sérieux)
l. Sa peau est .... (doux)
m. Ses parents sont .... (ambitieux)
n. La pollution est .... (affreux)
o. Mes grand-parents sont .... (vieux)
p. La réponse est .... (faux)
q. Ma tante n'est pas .... (généreux)
r. Ces histoires sont .... (ennuyeux)
s. Mes notes sont .... (affreux)
t. ...... Noël! (joyeux)

Adjectives which end in -s, -n or -l

These usually double the final consonant before adding **-e**.

meaning	singular		plural	
	masculine	**feminine**	**masculine**	**feminine**
low fat/big	bas gros	basse grosse	bas gros	basses grosses
good old	bon ancien	bonne ancienne	bons anciens	bonnes anciennes
kind/nice natural	gentil naturel	gentille naturelle	gentils naturels	gentilles naturelles

Adjectives which end in -eau

meaning	singular		plural	
	masculine	**feminine**	**masculine**	**feminine**
beautiful/ good looking	beau (bel*)	belle	beaux	belles
new	nouveau (nouvel*)	nouvelle	nouveaux	nouvelles

* Before masculine nouns beginning with a vowel or silent **h**, **beau** becomes **bel** and **nouveau** becomes **nouvel**: **un bel/nouvel hôtel**.

Adjectives which end in -ng

These add **u** before the **-e**.

long	long	longue	longs	longues

V Give the right form of the adjectives in brackets.

a. Mon oncle est .... (gros)
b. Ma tante n'est pas .... (gros)
c. Ma petite sœur est .... (gentil)
d. Mes parents ne sont pas .... (gentil)
e. Ma grande sœur est .... (beau)
f. Son ami n'est pas .... (beau)
g. Mes amies sont .... (bon)
h. Mes grands-parents sont .... (bon)
i. Buvez de l'eau ...... ! (naturel)
j. Les images sont .... (naturel)
k. Avignon est une ville .... (ancien)
l. M. Hibert est un ...... professeur de géographie. (ancien)
m. La Haye est la capitale des Pays .... (bas)

n. La chaise est trop .... (bas)
o. C'est un ...... livre. (nouveau)
p. Il y a un ...... hôtel dans cette rue. (nouveau)
q. Les ...... maisons sont dans la rue Lecourbe. (nouveau)
r. Quelle ...... vue! (beau)
s. Nous avons une ...... voiture. (nouveau)
t. Mes notes sont .... (bon)

Adjectives which end in -er

The feminine forms take a grave accent.

meaning	singular		plural	
	masculine	**feminine**	**masculine**	**feminine**
dear/ expensive	cher	chère	chers	chères
proud	fier	fière	fiers	fières
last	dernier	dernière	derniers	dernières
first	premier	première	premiers	première

Adjectives which end in -c

meaning	singular		plural	
	masculine	**feminine**	**masculine**	**feminine**
dry	sec	sèche	secs	sèches
white	blanc	blanche	blancs	blanches
Greek	grec	grecque	grecs	grecques
public	public	publique	publics	publiques

VI Give the right form of the adjectives in brackets.

a. C'est le ...... jour des vacances. (premier)
b. C'est la ...... fois que je vais en France. (premier)
c. La semaine ...... nous sommes allés à New York. (dernier)
d. Avez-vous vu le ...... film de Gérard Depardieu? (dernier)
e. Mes cheveux sont trop .... (sec)
f. J'ai les mains .... (sec)
g. Il préfère le vin .... (blanc)
h. Elle porte des sandales .... (blanc)
i. Sa chemise est .... (blanc)
j. Mes ...... amis. (cher)
k. Ma ...... amie. (cher)
l. Mon ami est très ...... de sa moto. (fier)
m. Ses parents sont très ...... de lui. (fier)

n. C'est la . . . . . . tarte aux fraises. (dernier)
o. Il a mangé le . . . . . . croissant. (dernier)
p. On a trouvé un ancien vase . . . . (grec)
q. Les îles . . . . . . sont très belles. (grec)
r. On va au jardin . . . . (public)
s. La piscine . . . . . . n'est pas encore ouverte. (public)
t. Il préfère un vin . . . . (sec)
u. Il voyage en . . . . . . classe. (premier)
v. Les cheveux de mon grand-père sont . . . . (blanc)

4.2 Adjectives of colour

Most adjectives of colour agree in the same way as other adjectives, and they always come after the noun they describe.

4.2.1 Regular adjectives

*Remember that the plural **-s** is not pronounced and most forms of the adjectives of colour will sound the same except for **vert/verte** and **blanc/blanche**.*

Adjectives of colour form their agreements in the same way as adjectives, including those which end in **-e** and **-c** (see 4.1.1 and 4.1.2).

	singular		**plural**	
meaning	**masculine**	**feminine**	**masculine**	**feminine**
black	noir	noire	noirs	noires
blue	bleu	bleue	bleus	bleues
green	vert	verte	verts	vertes
red	rouge	rouge	rouges	rouges
yellow	jaune	jaune	jaunes	jaunes
white	blanc	blanche	blancs	blanches

Adjectives of colour always come after the noun.

La Maison Blanche, la robe noire, les chemises bleues

I Complete the sentences with the right form of the colour given in brackets.

a. Sandrine porte une jupe . . . . (rouge)
b. Ses sandales sont . . . . (vert)

c. Matthias porte une chemise . . . . (gris)
d. Sa gabardine est . . . . (bleu)
e. Kathy porte une robe du soir . . . . (bleu)
f. Ses chaussures sont . . . . (rouge)
g. Simon porte un tee-shirt . . . . (jaune)
h. Ses espadrilles sont . . . . (rouge)
i. Jennifer porte un tailleur-pantalon . . . . (bleu)
j. Ses bottes en caoutchouc sont . . . . (jaune)

4.2.2 Adjectives of colour which don't change

- Adjectives made up of two words.
  bleu marine, bleu pâle, bleu clair, bleu foncé
- Nouns which are being used as adjectives.

brown (chestnut)	marron, marron, marron, marron
ivory	ivoire, ivoire, ivoire, ivoire
(parma) violet	parme, parme, parme, parme
chocolate	chocolat, chocolat, chocolat, chocolat

When two colour words are used together, they are hyphenated.
bleu-vert, bleu-gris

II Add the correct form of the adjective given in brackets.
a. Séverine a les yeux . . . . (bleu-vert)
b. . . . et des cheveux . . . . (marron)
c. Elle porte un sarong . . . . . . , . . . (bleu marine)
d. . . . un bustier . . . . (ivoire)
e. . . . et un cardigan . . . . (parme)
f. Ses mocassions sont . . . . (bleu clair)
g. . . . et ses chaussettes . . . . (blanc)
h. Les murs de son atelier de peintre sont . . . . (rose pâle)
i. . . . les rideaux sont . . . . (rose foncé)
j. . . . et la porte est . . . . (turquoise)

4.3 The position of adjectives

Most adjectives and all adjectives of colour come after the noun . . .
la maison moderne, le garçon paresseux
. . . although in French, some adjectives do come in front of the noun they qualify/describe.
la petite maison, le grand bâtiment

The adjectives which do come in front of the noun are **beau**, **bon**, **demi**, **grand**, **gros**, **jeune**, **joli**, **long**, **mauvais**, **prochain***, **vieux**.

I Put these adjectives in the right place.

a. une enterprise (jeune)
b. une jacinthe (bleue)
c. un enfant (sage)
d. un bijou (petit)
e. une femme (belle)
f. un après-midi (paresseux)
g. un château (vieux)
h. une idée (bonne)
i. un chat (petit/noir)
j. un rat (gros)
k. une histoire (intéressante)
l. une couleur (jolie)
m. une erreur (grosse)
n. un philosophe (moderne)
o. un film (ennuyeux)
p. un voyage (long)
q. une expérience (mauvaise)
r. une ville (grande)
s. des falaises (blanches)
t. un penseur (nouveau)

4.4 Adjectives with two meanings

Some adjectives have a completely different meaning depending on whether they are used in front of or after the noun.

un cher ami	a dear friend
un pullover cher	an expensive pullover
un ancien élève	a former pupil
une ville ancienne	an old town
mes propres mains	my own hands
des mains propres	clean hands
Ce pauvre enfant!	That poor child!
une famille pauvre	a poor family
le seul homme au monde	the only man in the world
L'homme seul près de la porte est M. Beguin.	The man on his own by the door is Mr Beguin.

I Put the adjective in the right place in the sentence according to the context.

a. M. Gilbert l'a vu de ses yeux. (propres)
b. Je vais vous présenter, auditeurs, un auteur contemporain. (chers)
c. Jérôme est un élève de mon lycée. (ancien)
d. Je n'ai plus de chaussettes. (propres)
e. La voiture la plus est une Ferrari. (chère)
f. Mon oncle nous a montré la ville. (ancienne)

* When used with days of the week, months and years, **prochain(e)** comes after the noun. See 4.4 for other adjectives that can occur in both positions.

g. Des millions de cailles sont tuées chaque année pendant la saison de la chasse. (pauvres)
h. Les familles habitent dans des bidonvilles. (pauvres)
i. La solution, c'est d'aller voir par vous-même. (seule)
j. L'homme qui attend le bus, c'est M. Robert. (seul)

4.5 The comparative

The comparative is the form you use when you are comparing two things and say, for example, that something is bigger, smaller, newer, older, etc.

4.5.1 The comparative in French

In French, you put **plus** (*more*) or **moins** (*less*) in front of the adjective.

M. Bertrand est important. Le P.D.G.* est plus important.	Mr Bertrand is important. The MD is more important.
Marc est petit. Sa sœur est plus petite.	Marc is small. His sister is smaller.
Fabien est intelligent. Son frère est moins intelligent.	Fabien is intelligent. His brother is less intelligent.

The adjective still agrees with the noun it describes.

I Say the second things are all 'more' than the first.
a. Nicolas est timide mais sa sœur est *plus timide.*
b. Notre maison est grande mais votre maison est ....
c. Cet exercice est difficile mais l'exercice suivant est ....
d. L'article du *Nouvel économiste* est intéressant mais l'émission sur C4 est ....
e. Le mont Blanc est haut mais le mont Everest est ....
f. La Seine est longue mais le Rhône est ....

II Now say the second things are all 'less' than the first.
a. Une Mercedes est chère mais une Citroën est ....
b. La banque X est grande mais la banque Y est ....
c. L'équipe A est bonne mais l'équipe B est ....
d. L'émission 1 est intéressante mais l'émission 2 est ....

* P.D.G. = Président directeur général.

4.5.2 Comparing two things

When you say something is bigger *than* something else, you use **que**.

Il est plus grand que moi.	He is bigger than me.
Il est moins intelligent que son frère.	He is less intelligent than his brother.

4.5.3 Saying *as . . . as*

If you are comparing two things which are similar, you use the expression **aussi (grand(e)) que** (*as (big) as*).

Il est aussi grand que son père.	He is as big as his father.
Il est aussi étrange que son frère.	He is as strange as his brother.

III Say these places are bigger (+), smaller (−) or as big as (=). (Remember to make grand **agree with the noun where necessary.)**

a. L'Hôtel Bellevue est . . . . . . l'Hôtel Bijou. (−)
b. Paris est . . . . . . Lyon. (+)
c. M. Bricolage est . . . . . . Lacroix. (=)
d. L'hypermarché Champion est . . . . . . Continent. (−)
e. Le lac d'Annecy est . . . . . . le lac du Bourget. (−)
f. La Tour Eiffel est . . . . . . que Blackpool Tower. (+)

IV Make these things more, less or just as . . . as.

a. Le mont Everest est . . . . . . le Kilimanjaro. (+ haut)
b. La Seine est . . . . . . la Loire. (− long)
c. En Afrique, il fait . . . . . . en Europe. (+ chaud)
d. La vue de la montagne est . . . . . . la vue du lac. (= beau)
e. Le footing est . . . . . . le yoga. (+ fatigant)

4.5.4 Good, better

	masculine	**feminine**
singular	bon, meilleur	bonne, meilleure
plural	bons, meilleurs	bonnes, meilleures

V How would you say these things are better?

a. Le vin rouge est bon mais le vin blanc est . . . .
b. Les chaussures sont bonnes mais les sandales sont . . . .
c. La Citroën est bonne mais la Mercedes est . . . .
d. Les spaghettis sont bons mais les canellonis sont . . . .
e. Le café est bon mais le chocolat est . . . .
f. Les filles sont bonnes mais les garçons sont . . . .
g. Cette année, mon fils a de . . . . . . notes.
h. On attend de . . . . . . nouvelles de l'hôpital.

***Bon(s)** and **bonne(s)** do sound different, but **meilleur(s)** and **meilleure(s)** sound nearly the same.*

4.6 The superlative

You use the superlative when you are comparing more than two things. You use it to say something is the biggest, the smallest, the best or the worst, etc.

Mont Blanc is the highest mountain in Europe.
Cantona is the best footballer.

4.6.1 The superlative in French

In French, as in English, you add the definite article to the comparative form.

Nicolas est grand, Ludovic est plus grand mais Stéphane est le plus grand.	Nicolas is big, Ludovic is bigger but Stéphane is the biggest.
Marianne est petite, Grégoire est plus petit mais Mathieu est le plus petit.	Marianne is small, Grégoire is smaller but Mathieu is the smallest.

Also as in English, if you are talking about someone's best friend/worst experience/etc., **mon/ma/mes**, etc. can be used instead of the definite article.

ma plus grande crainte	my biggest fear
leur plus grand désir	their dearest wish
notre plus petit chat	our smallest cat

I Put the adjectives in brackets into the correct form of the superlative.

a. La montagne ...... d'Europe est le Mont Blanc. (+ haut)
b. Le fleuve ...... de France est la Loire. (+ long)
c. La grotte ...... s'appelle le puits d'Aphanize. (+ profond)
d. Le stalagmite ...... se trouve dans Armand. (+ grand)
e. Le réseau de grottes ...... s'appelle Félix Trombe et s'étend sur 70 km. (+ long)
f. Le glacier ...... d'Europe s'appelle le glacier d'Argentière. (+ long)
g. Le lac naturel ...... de France est le lac du Bourget. (+ grand)
h. L'acteur français ...... s'appelle Gérard Depardieu. (+ connu)
i. L'arbre vivant ...... a 4 700 ans. (+ vieux)
j. L'animal qui a la morsure ...... est un requin noir. (+ fort)

4.6.2 Irregular superlatives: good, better, best

As with *good* in English, **bon** has an irregular comparative and superlative form.

adjective	comparative	superlative
bon good	meilleur better	le meilleur best

Simon est bon joueur de bridge.	Simon is a good bridge player.
Thomas est meilleur joueur de bridge que Simon.	Thomas is a better bridge player than Simon.
Boris est le meilleur joueur de bridge.	Boris is the best bridge player.
Sandrine est la meilleure joueuse de bridge.	Sandrine is the best bridge player.

II Add the correct form (meilleur/meilleure/meilleurs/meilleures).

a. C'est mon ...... parapluie. Ne le perdez pas!
b. C'est ma ...... photo de mon ami.
c. Ma ...... amie s'appelle Céline.
d. La vue d'ici est la ...... de la région.
e. Cette église est le ...... exemple d'une église romane en France.

4.7 Possessive adjectives: *my, your, his, her, etc.*

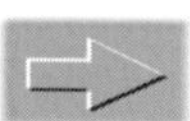

If you know all about possessive adjectives, go on to 4.8.

Possessive adjectives are words which tell you to whom something belongs: ***my** coat*, ***his** umbrella*, ***your** briefcase*, ***their** house*, ***our** cat*, etc. These are important words that we don't usually think of as adjectives, but they 'describe' a noun so they are classed as adjectives.

In English, we only have one form of each: *my*, *your*, *his*, *her*, *our*, *their*. In French, the possessive adjective has to agree with the noun it is describing.

4.7.1 Possessive adjectives in French

	masculine	feminine	plural
my	mon	ma	mes
your (tu)	ton	ta	tes
his/her	son	sa	ses
our	notre	notre	nos
your (vous)	votre	votre	vos
their	leur	leur	leurs

4.7.2 My (*mon, ma, mes*)

The word for *my* agrees with the person or thing it is describing. This means that you use the masculine form (**mon**) with masculine nouns.

mon frère — my brother
mon portable — my mobile
mon ami — my friend

My in front of feminine nouns is **ma**.

ma sœur — my sister
ma voiture — my car

But you use **mon** in front of feminine nouns which begin with a vowel. This is because it is easier to say. However, if there is another word between them, e.g. **petite**, it goes back to being **ma**.

mon amie — my (female) friend
ma petite amie — my girlfriend

You use the plural form **mes** with plural nouns.

mes parents — my parents
mes amis, mes amies — my friends

I Mon, ma **or** mes?

a. …… ordinateur
b. …… clés
c. …… mobile
d. …… agenda
e. …… crayon
f. …… dossier
g. …… courrier
h. …… carte bancaire
i. …… ticket de bus
j. …… porte-monnaie

II Now do the same for your clothes . . .

a. …… pantalon
b. …… chemise
c. …… pull
d. …… chaussettes
e. …… chaussures
f. …… anorak
g. …… manteau
h. …… écharpe
i. …… gants
j. …… parapluie

III . . . and your family. Imagine you are showing someone photographs of your family. What would you say?

C'est mon/ma . . ./Ce sont mes . . .

a. enfants
b. mari
c. femme
d. père
e. mère
f. sœur
g. frères
h. grands-parents
i. cousin
j. fils
k. fille

4.7.3 Your (*ton, ta, tes*)

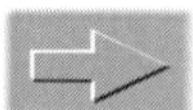

If you are not going to need the* ton *form (it behaves just like the* mon *form), go on to 4.7.4.

The words for *your* (**ton**, **ta**, **tes**) rhyme with the words for *my* (**mon**, **ma**, **mes**) and behave in the same way.

IV Put the correct form of ton, ta **or** tes **in front of these words.**

C'est ton/ta . . ./Ce sont tes . . .

a. enfants
b. père
c. mère
d. sœurs
e. frère
f. grands-parents
g. fille
h. fils
i. chiens
j. chat

V How would you ask what they are called?

Comment s'appelle ton/ta . . . ?/Comment s'appellent tes . . . ?

a. collègues
b. collègue
c. copain
d. copines
e. amis
f. amies
g. ami
h. amie
i. petite amie
j. petit ami

4.7.4 His and her (*son, sa, ses*)

The words for *his/her* also rhyme with **mon**, **ma**, **mes** and **ton**, **ta**, **tes** and are used in the same way. Notice that **son frère** means *his/her brother*, **sa sœur** means *his/her sister* and **ses parents** means *his/her parents*.

VI Parlez-moi de Thomas. **Tell me about Thomas by filling in the right word** (son, sa, ses)**.**

a. . . . . . . amie s'appelle Juliette.
b. . . . . . . cousin s'appelle Auban.
c. . . . . . . frère est grand.
d. . . . . . . mère est sculpteur.
e. . . . . . . père travaille à la BCE (Banque Centrale Européenne).

f. ...... sœur fait de la recherche en cardiologie.
g. ...... petit frère n'a que dix ans.
h. ...... sport préféré est le tennis.
i. ...... plat préféré est la pizza 'Quatre saisons'.
j. ...... couleur préférée est le rouge coquelicot.

VII Parlez-moi de Charlotte. **Now do the same for Charlotte's family and friends.**

a. ...... amie s'appelle Jennifer.
b. ...... petit ami s'appelle Benjamin.
c. ...... frère s'appelle Nicolas.
d. ...... sœur s'appelle Isabelle.
e. Comment s'appellent ...... parents?
f. ...... scooter est noir et jaune.
g. ...... passion, c'est le théâtre.
h. ...... couleur préférée est le bleu.
i. ...... plat préféré est le filet de veau Marengo.
j. ...... boisson préférée est un cocktail à base de champagne.

4.7.5 Our (*notre/nos*)

The word for *our* is **notre**. It is the same for both masculine and feminine, but changes to **nos** in the pural: **notre appartement**, **notre maison**, **nos enfants**.

VIII How would you say these are *our* things?

C'est notre . . ./Ce sont nos . . .

a. maison
b. appartement
c. balcon
d. cave
e. vins
f. garage
g. voiture
h. jardin
i. arbres
j. pelouse

4.7.6 Your (*votre/vos*)

The word for *your* (**vous** form) is easy to remember because it rhymes with **notre** and **nos** and behaves in the same way: **votre appartement**, **votre maison**, **vos enfants**.

IX Ask if these are *your* things.

C'est votre . . . ?/Ce sont vos . . . ?

a. bureau
b. chaise
c. ordinateur
d. papiers
e. manteau
f. gants
g. parapluie
h. affaires
i. portefeuille
j. clés

4.7.7 Their (*leur/leurs*)

The word for *their* is **leur**. It adds an **-s** in the plural: **leur appartement**, **leur maison**, **leurs enfants**.

X Say these are their things.

C'est leur . . ./Ce sont leurs . . .

a. voiture
b. garage
c. vélos
d. jardin
e. fleurs
f. plantes
g. maison
h. porte
i. fenêtres
j. balcon

4.7.8 Quickie

- *Mon*, *ma* and *mes*, etc. agree with the words they describe.
- If a female noun begins with a vowel, you use *mon/ton/son* instead of *ma/ta/sa*.
- *Son*, *sa* and *ses* mean both his and hers.
- *Notre*, *votre* and *leur* become *nos*, *vos* and *leurs* in the plural.

4.8 Demonstrative adjectives

The demonstrative adjective points out a particular thing or things.
this page, that book, these clothes

4.8.1 Demonstrative adjectives in French

singular		**plural**
masculine	**feminine**	
ce (cet*)	cette	ces

* You use **cet** before a masculine noun which begins with a vowel or silent **h**.

I Put the correct form (ce, cet, cette **or** ces) **in front of these words.**

a. Je vous conseille ...... hôtel.
b. Derrière ...... maison il y a un grand jardin.
c. Dans ...... jardin il y a beaucoup de plantes exotiques.
d. ...... personnes travaillent dans le jardin.
e. ...... fleurs sont rares.
f. ...... arbre est très vieux.
g. ...... porte est pour les visiteurs.
h. ...... dépliants sont gratuits.
i. ...... homme prend des photos.
j. Il est défendu de prendre des photos au cours de la visite de ...... musée.

4.8.2 This/that/these/those

To differentiate between things that are close to you (*this/these*) and things that are further away (*that/those*), you add **-ci** or **-là** to the noun.

ce chien-ci	this dog
ce chien-là	that dog
cette fleur-ci	this flower
cette fleur-là	that flower
ces gants-ci	these gloves
ces gants-là	those gloves

*To remember which is which, think of **ici** (here) and **là** (there).*

4.9 Interrogative adjectives

The interrogative adjective *which* is translated in French by **quel**, which agrees with the noun.

singular		**plural**	
masculine	**feminine**	**masculine**	**feminine**
quel	quelle	quels	quelles

I Put in the correct form: quel, quelle, quels **or** quelles.

a Which hotel would you prefer? Vous préférez ...... hôtel?
b. Which room would you prefer? Vous préférez ...... chambre?
c. Which table do you prefer? Vous préférez ...... table?
d. Which flowers do you prefer? Vous préférez ...... fleurs?
e. Which address should I send it to? Je l'envoie à ...... adresse?

f.	Which flat do you live in?	Vous habitez . . . . . . appartement?
g.	I don't know which coat to wear.	Je ne sais pas . . . . . . manteau porter.
h.	Which shoes are you going to wear?	. . . . . . chaussures allez-vous porter?

4.10 Indefinite adjectives

These adjectives agree as normal with the noun (but note that some, such as **plusieurs** and **quelques**, are only used in the plural).

autre (*other*)

Je vais prendre une autre route. — I am going to take another road.
Connaissez-vous des autres histoires? — Do you know any other stories?

certain (*certain*)

Cette opération demande un certain savoir-faire. — This procedure demands a certain competence.
Il y a une certaine émission que je regarde tous les jours. — There is a certain programme I watch every day.

chaque (*each/every*)

chaque jour — each day
chaque fois — every time

même (*same*)

en même temps — at the same time
je vois les mêmes gens dans le bureau. — I see the same people in the office.

plusieurs (*some*)

J'y suis allé plusieurs fois. — I have been (there) several times.

quelques (*a few*)

Avez-vous quelques minutes? — Have you got a few minutes?

tout (*all*)

tout le temps — all the time
toute ma famille — all my family
tous les autres — all the others
toutes les fleurs — all the flowers

Adverbs

Adverbs are words which describe a verb.

She drives *fast*. He speaks *too loudly*.

Some adverbs can qualify an adjective or adverb, e.g. *very*, *quite*, *too*.

5.1 Formation of adverbs

5.1.1 Regular adverbs

Most French adverbs are formed by adding **-ment** to the feminine form of the adjective.

douce → doucement	quietly/softly
lent → lentement	slowly
traditionnelle → traditionnellement	traditionally
normale → normalement	normally/usually
regulière → regulièrement	regularly

5.1.2 Adjectives ending in *-ent* and *-ant*

These change the ending to **-emment** or **-amment**. The only exception is **lent** (see above).

évident → évidemment	evidently
constant → constamment	constantly
récent → récemment	recently

5.1.3 Adverbs to watch

adjective	adverb
bon – good mauvais – bad continu – continuous gentil – nice petit – little meilleur – better	bien – well mal – badly continûment – continuously gentiment – nicely peu – few mieux – better

5.2 Adjectives used as adverbs

Some adjectives can be used as adverbs in certain contexts.

- when talking about speaking/singing/playing an instrument

fort	loud/strong
parler fort	to talk loudly
haut	high
chanter haut	to sing high
bas	low
parler bas	to speak in a low voice

- When talking about prices

cher	dear
Ça coûte cher.	It is expensive.

- When saying whether something is true or false

vrai	true
C'est vrai.	It's true.
faux	false
C'est faux.	It's wrong/false.

- In certain other situations

dur	hard
C'est dur.	It's hard/difficult.
court	short
couper court	to cut short
net	neat/tidy
refuser net	to refuse point blank

I How would you say?

a. Speak more slowly, please! Parlez plus . . . . . . , s'il vous plaît!
b. He refused point blank.
c. That's not true!
d. It's too expensive.
e. Speak more loudly, please.

5.3 Other useful adverbs

The following adverbs are very common, so it's worth learning them.

très – very
assez – quite
trop – too
souvent – frequently/often

5.4 The comparative and superlative of adverbs

The comparative and superlative forms of adverbs are made like the comparative and superlative of adjectives, using **plus** or **le plus**, etc.

Lire, c'est difficile.	Reading is difficult.
Comprendre, c'est plus difficile.	Understanding is more difficult.
Parler, c'est le plus difficile.	Speaking is the most difficult.

The following adverbs have irregular comparative and superlative forms.

adverb	**comparative**	**superlative**
beaucoup	plus	le plus
peu	moins	le moins
bien	mieux	le mieux

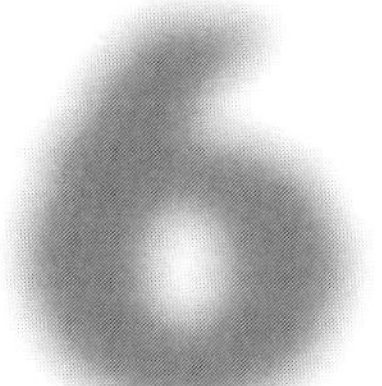

Prepositions

6.1 Recognising prepositions

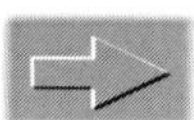

If you know what a preposition is go on to 6.2.

Prepositions are words like *in*, *on*, and *under*. Unlike adjectives, they do not change. They are usually used in conjunction with a noun or pronoun, e.g. *in the cupboard*, *near the station*, *for her*, *with me*.

Prepositions can tell you:

- where a person or thing is, i.e. its position

sur la table	on the table
sous le pont	under the bridge

- how something is done, i.e. manner

avec du beurre	with butter
sans eau	without water

- when something happens, i.e. time

dans une minute	in a minute
après le dîner	after dinner

- for whom something is done

pour moi	for me

6.2 The preposition à

6.2.1 Uses of à

À is a very useful preposition. It can be used to convey position, manner, time and possession according to the context in which it is used.

Position

Il habite à la campagne.	He lives in the country.
Pour aller à la gare?	To get to the station?

Manner/sort

un sandwich au jambon	a ham sandwich
un homme aux cheveux longs	a man with long hair

Time

Le train part à 10h45.	The train leaves at 10.45.

Possession

C'est à moi!	It's mine!

6.2.2 *À* and the definite article

When **à** is used in front of the definite article and a noun, it combines with the article to make **au** in the masculine singular and **aux** in the plural.

masculine	**feminine**	**plural**
à + le → au	à + la → à la	à + les → aux

Je vais au cinéma chaque semaine.	I go to the cinema every week.
Mon frère aime aller aux marchés.	My brother likes going to the markets.

6.2.3 *À* meaning *at* or *to*

This is usually in answer to the question **où** (*where*).

Je suis à la maison.	I am at home.
Je vais au bureau.	I am going to the office.

I How would you say you were going to these places?

Je vais à . . .

a. la plage
b. le bureau
c. l'hôtel
d. le marché
e. le musée
f. la banque
g. l'hôpital
h. l'aéroport
i. le distributeur (cash point)
j. la gare

6.2.4 *À* used with towns and countries

À is also used with:

- the names of all towns
- the names of countries which are masculine, unless they begin with a vowel
- the names of all countries and regions which include **les** in their name
  au Canada, au Luxembourg, aux États-Unis

*You use **en** with all feminine names of countries and ones which begin with a vowel.*
en Angleterre ***en France***

II How would you say where these places are?

a. La Tour Eiffel est . . . . . . Paris.
b. Buckingham Palace est . . . . . . Londres.
c. L'Empire State Building est . . . . . . États-Unis.
d. Montréal est . . . . . . Canada.
e. Tokyo est . . . . . . Japon.
f. La Cour européenne de justice se trouve . . . . . . Luxembourg.
g. La Haye est . . . . . . Pays-Bas.
h. La Guadeloupe est . . . . . . Antilles.
i. On parle français . . . . . . Québec.
j. Lisbonne est . . . . . . Portugal.

*The rule for **à** + definite article applies with the names of towns:*
***à** + **le** → **au** and **à** + **les** → **aux**.*

III How would you say you are going to these places?

Je vais à . . .

a. Le Havre
b. Le Mans
c. les Champs-Elysées
d. les Deux-Alpes
e. le Lavandou
f. le Louvre
g. les Menuires
h. la Cité des Sciences et de l'Industrie

6.2.5 *À* used in answer to the question: What kind of?

Notice that when you are saying what kind of sandwich, cake, ice cream, etc. you want, you have to add **au/à l'/à la/à l'** or **aux** in French where there is no word in English.

Quelle sorte de sandwich voulez-vous?	What sort of sandwich would you like?
Un sandwich au fromage.	A cheese sandwich.
Une glace quel parfum?	What flavour ice cream?
Une glace au chocolat.	A chocolate ice cream.

IV How would you ask for these sandwiches?

Je voudrais un sandwich à . . .

a. le jambon
b. le fromage
c. la banane
d. la confiture
e. les tomates
f. le thon
g. le lard
h. le saucisson

6.2.6 *À* used in expressions of power

À is used in these expressions.

à essence	petrol
à vent	wind powered
à propulsion nucléaire	nuclear powered

Remember that the final ***-x*** *in* ***aux*** *is not pronounced . . .*
une tarte aux fraises, une glace aux cerises, une omelette aux fines herbes
. . . unless it is followed by a word beginning with a vowel, and then it makes a liaison, the z sound being carried on to the beginning of the next word.
un flan aux‿asperges, une quiche aux‿épinards, un gâteau aux‿amandes

6.3 The preposition *de*

6.3.1 *De* and the definite article

When **de** is used in front of the definite article, it combines to make **du** in the masculine singular and **des** in the plural.

masculine	**feminine**	**plural**
de + le → du	de + la → de la	de + les → des

6.3.2 Uses of *de*

De can mean:

- *of*
  C'est le centre de la ville. — It's the centre of the town.
- *from*
  M. Bériot arrive de la gare. — Mr Bériot is coming from the station.
- *than*
  Maurice a plus de vingt ans et moins de trente ans. — Maurice is more than twenty and less than thirty years old.
- *with/in*
  La voiture est couverte de boue. — The car is covered in mud.

I Complete these sentences using de **and the phrase in brackets.**

a. Les touristes arrivent .... (le Japon)
b. Ils descendent .... (le train)
c. Ils font un tour .... (les monuments)
d. Ils visitent le musée .... (le Louvre)
e. Ils traversent la place .... (la Concorde)
f. Ils prennent le pont .... (Bir-Hakeim)
g. Ils prennent des photos .... (la Tour Eiffel)
h. Leur hôtel est près .... (la place du Trocadéro)

6.3.3 *De* meaning some (of)

Where English uses *some (of)*, French needs **de** plus the definite article.

Je voudrais du beurre, de la confiture et des cerises. — I'd like some butter, some jam and some cherries.

See also 2.4.

II Tony prépare le dîner. **What does he need? Remember that in negative sentences, you use** de **without the article.**

a. J'ai besoin ...... (le jambon), ...
b. .... (les pommes de terre), ...
c. .... (les tomates) ...
d. ... et ...... (la salade).
e. Nous n'avons plus ...... (les tomates).
f. Je veux ...... (la moutarde), ...
g. .... (l'huile), ...
h. .... (le sel) ...
i. ... et ...... (le poivre) pour faire une mayonnaise.

6.3.4 *De* in expressions of quantity

In these expressions, the **de** does not change.

un kilo de	a kilo of
un kilo de pommes de terre	a kilo of potatoes
une bouteille de	a bottle of
une bouteille de ketchup	a bottle of ketchup
une boîte de	a tin/can of
une boîte de sardines	a tin of sardines
un lot de	a pack of/special offer of
un lot de trois savons	a pack of three soaps
un litre de	a litre of
un litre de lait	a litre of milk

III Au restaurant. **How would you ask for these?**

a. 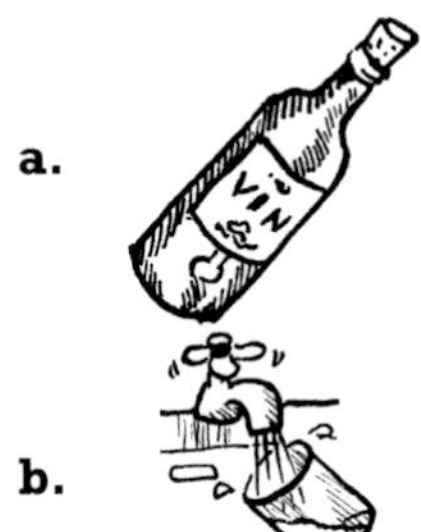

d.  

g.  

b. 

e. 

h. 

c. 

f.

You also use **de** in the following expressions of quantity. Again, the **de** does not change.

assez de	enough (of)
Il a assez d'argent.	He has enough money.
beaucoup de	a lot of
J'ai beaucoup de travail.	I have a lot of work.
peu de	a little
un peu de sel	a little salt
plus de	more (of)
Il a plus d'argent.	He has more money.
moins de	less
Elle a moins d'argent que son partenaire.	She has less money than her business partner.
trop de	too many (of)
Elle fait trop de fautes.	She makes too many mistakes.

See also 2.4.3.

6.4 Prepositions of position

Prepositions which tell you position (where something or somebody is) include the following.

dans	in
dans la maison	in the house
derrière	behind
derrière la porte	behind the door
devant	in front of
devant le cinéma	in front of the cinema
entre	between
entre le cinéma et le café	between the cinema and the café
sous	under
sous le pont	under the bridge
sur	on
sur la table	on the table

I Où est Jean-Pierre? **Match the picture with the sentence.**

a. Il est sous la douche. **1.**

b. Il est derrière la porte de la salle de bains. **2.**

c. Il est devant la glace. **3.**

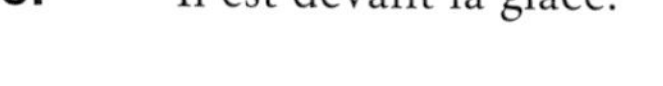

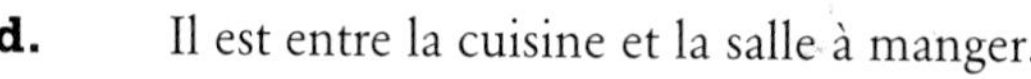

d. Il est entre la cuisine et la salle à manger. **4.**

e. Il est sur son lit. **5.**

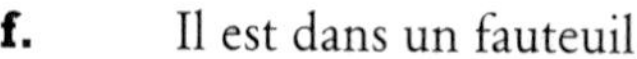

f. Il est dans un fauteuil. **6.**

II What you would say to tell someone where the telephone is?

Il y a un téléphone . . .

6.5 The prepositions *en* and *chez*

En translates *in* when you are talking about countries which are feminine or begin with a vowel.

Elle habite en Espagne.	She lives in Spain.

Chez is a special preposition which means *at the house of.* It is followed by the person's name or the relevant emphatic pronoun (**moi**, **toi**, **lui**, **elle**, **nous**, **vous**, **elles**, **eux**).

chez moi	at my house
chez lui	at his/her house

6.6 Useful prepositional phrases

These tell you where something or someone is. They are called phrases because they are made up of more than one word, e.g. *in front of* is a prepositional phrase in English because it is made up of three words.

Remember that:
de** + **le** becomes **du
de** + **la** does not change: **de la
de** + **l'** does not change: **de l'
de** + **les** becomes **des

en face de	opposite
près de	near
loin de	far from
à côté de	beside/next to
au-dessus de	above
au-dessous de	below/beneath
autour de	around

The following useful expressions tell you where someone or something is in a building.

en haut	upstairs
en bas	downstairs
au rez de chaussée	on the ground floor
au premier/deuxième étage	on the first/second floor
au sous-sol	in the basement

6.7 Expressions of time

These tell you when something happened.

à	at
à dix heures	at ten o'clock
après	after
après le petit déjeuner	after breakfast
avant	before
avant d'aller au bureau	before going to the office
pendant	during
pendant la journée	during the day
pour	for
pour une semaine	for a week (in the future)
vers	about

vers dix heures	about/towards ten o'clock
depuis	since
Je t'attends depuis ce matin.	I've been waiting for you since this morning.

The French use ***depuis*** *(since) when in English we often use 'for'.* *See 1.22.1 for verb tenses with* ***depuis****.*

Il habite ici depuis trois ans.	He has been living here for three years.
Depuis combien de temps prenez-vous des cours de français?	How long have you been studying French (and you still are)?
Je prends des cours de français depuis deux ans.	I have been doing it (and I still am) for two years.

I How would you answer these questions, using the information given in brackets?

Depuis combien de temps . . .

a. . . . Marc prend-il des cours d'espagnol? (deux ans)
b. . . . habite-t-il à Paris? (cinq ans)
c. . . . M. Proudhon habite-t-il à Paris? (deux mois)
d. . . . joue-t-il de la guitare? (un an)
e. . . . travaille-t-il dans cette boulangerie? (six mois)
f. . . . joue-t-il aux échecs? (son enfance)
g. . . . Constance est-elle végetarienne? (l'âge de treize ans)
h. . . . fait-elle du ski? (cinq ans)
i. . . . font-ils de la planche? (l'été dernier)
j. . . . regardent-ils des films de science fiction? (trois ans)
k. . . . sortent-ils ensemble? (six mois)

7

Conjunctions and other useful noises

Here are some useful words for joining two parts of a sentence or filling in gaps in a conversation.

et	and
mais	but
puis	then
alors	then, so
en tout cas	anyway
eh ben . . .	well, er
et voilà	and there you are
voici	here is
oh là là	oh dear
C'est tout!	That's all!

And some other useful phrases.

Ne quittez pas.	Hold on. (on the telephone)
Veuillez patienter.	Please wait. (on the telephone)
Attendez.	Wait.
Je n'en sais rien.	I don't know anything about it.
Je m'en doute.	I should have known.
Ça m'étonnerait.	I find that surprising (I would be surprised if that were true).

1.1

I **a** parler *to speak* **b** habiter *to live* **c** organiser *to organise* **d** entrer *to enter* **e** voyager *to travel* **f** porter *to carry/wear* **g** vérifier *to verify/check* **h** inviter *to invite* **i** laver *to wash* **j** arriver *to arrive*

II **a** manger *to eat* **b** dîner *to dine* **c** déjeuner *to lunch* **d** apprécier *to appreciate* **e** goûter *to taste/try* **f** souper *to have supper* **g** verser *to pour* **h** déguster *to taste/sample* **i** consommer *to consume* **j** assaisonner *to season (add salt and pepper, etc.)* **k** mélanger *to mix*

1.2

I **a** 3/vend **b** 1/montr **c** 1/chant **d** 2/sort **e** 1/lav **f** 2/fin **g** 1/écout **h** 1/ferm **i** 2/part **j** 3/prend **k** 2/chois **l** 1/port **m** 1/rentr **n** 2/ven **o** 2/dorm

1.3

I **a** *eat* manger **b** *drink* boire **c** *sleep* dormir **d** *go* aller **e** *talk* parler **f** *do* faire **g** *understand* comprendre **h** *buy* acheter **i** *leave* partir **j** *finish* finir **k** *say* dire **l** *write* écrire **m** *read* lire **n** *follow* suivre **o** *listen* écouter

1.4

I **a** je **b** elle **c** il **d** nous **e** tu **f** vous **g** elles **h** ils

II **a** il **b** elle **c** il **d** ils **e** elles **f** elles **g** je **h** ils **i** ils **j** nous

1.5

I **a** parle **b** mange **c** porte **d** travaille **e** regarde **f** joue **g** aime **h** écoute **i** habite **j** décide

II **a** travaille **b** arrive **c** gare **d** entre **e** salue **f** monte **g** compose **h** entre **i** accroche **j** commence

IV **a** vais **b** achète **c** appelle **d** préfère **e** paie **f** envoie **g** espère **h** essaie **i** jette **j** lève

V **a** parle **b** habite **c** vais **d** arrive **e** appelle **f** entre **g** monte **h** dîne **i** envoie **j** pose **k** joue **l** gagne **m** téléphone **n** regarde

VI **a** remplir **b** finir **c** grossir **d** maigrir **e** choisir **f** réfléchir **g** ralentir **h** applaudir **i** vieillir **j** rougir

VIII **a** sors **b** finis **c** choisis **d** pars **e** grossis **f** dors **g** ralentis **h** réfléchis **i** remplis **j** vieillis

IX **a** Je viens **b** J'offre **c** Je découvre **d** Je tiens **e** Je couvre **f** J'ouvre

X **a** J'ai **b** Je dois **c** Je sais **d** Je peux **e** Je dois **f** Je veux **g** Je vois **h** Je sais **i** J'ai

XI **a** Je vends **b** Je réponds **c** Je descends **d** J'attends **e** J'entends

XII **a** Je bois **b** J'écris **c** Je fais **d** Je lis **e** Je mets **f** Je suis **g** Je dis **h** Je décris **i** Je crois **j** Je prends

XIII **a** n'ai pas. **b** ne suis pas. **c** ne vais pas. **d** ne bois pas. **e** n'écris pas. **f** ne fais pas. **g** ne lis pas. **h** ne sais pas **i** ne vois pas **j** ne viens pas **k** ne peux pas **l** ne veux pas **m** ne mange pas **n** ne sors pas **o** ne regarde pas

XIV **a** Je me réveille **b** Je me lève **c** Je me lave **d** Je me douche. **e** Je m'habille. **f** Je m'assieds. **g** Je m'étonne. **h** Je m'ennuie. **i** Je me couche.

1.6

I **a** Nous travaillons aujourd'hui. **b** Nous jouons au volley ce soir. **c** Nous partons de la maison à 18h00. **d** Nous dînons au restaurant. **e** Nous rentrons à 22h00. **f** Nous allons à Paris demain. **g** Nous partons à 8h00. **h** Nous arrivons à 11h15. **i** Nous achetons nos billets à la gare. **j** Nous avons beaucoup de bagages.

II **a** parlons **b** voyons **c** choisissons **d** changeons **e** comprenons **f** allons **g** mangeons **h** prenons **i** travaillons **j** jouons

III **a** ne parlons pas **b** n'avons pas **c** n'allons pas **d** n'écrivons pas **e** n'avons pas **f** ne lisons pas **g** ne regardons pas **h** ne venons pas **i** ne buvons pas **j** n'avons pas **k** ne sommes pas **l** ne voyons pas

IV **a** Nous nous réveillons **b** Nous nous levons **c** Nous nous couchons **d** Nous nous douchons. **e** Nous nous reposons. **f** Nous nous dépêchons. **g** Nous nous habillons. **h** Nous nous lavons. **i** Nous nous promenons. **j** Nous nous séparons.

V **a** *we have* nous avons **b** *we are* nous sommes **c** *we are staying* nous restons **d** *we are eating* nous mangeons **e** *we can* nous pouvons **f** *we are not coming* nous ne venons pas **g** *we do not understand* nous ne comprenons pas **h** *we want* nous voulons **i** *we are going* nous allons **j** *we are seeing* nous voyons **k** *we are leaving* nous partons **l** *we are arriving* nous arrivons **m** *we are coming* nous venons **n** *we are doing* nous faisons **o** *we are reading* nous lisons

1.7

I **a** tu danses **b** tu aimes **c** tu habites **d** tu parles **e** tu regardes **f** tu manges **g** tu écoutes **h** tu joues **i** tu laves **j** tu travailles

II **a** es **b** as **c** aimes **d** manges **e** regardes **f** habites **g** parles **h** portes **i** fais **j** joues

III **a** Comment tu t'appelles? **b** Tu te lèves à quelle heure? **c** Tu te couches à quelle heure? **d** Tu t'intéresses aux animaux? **e** Tu ne t'intéresses pas à la musique?

IV **a** Tu as **b** Tu pars **c** Tu prends **d** Tu arrives **e** Tu dînes **f** Tu rentres

V **a** *Would you like a drink?* Tu veux boire quelque chose? **b** *Would you prefer a glass of wine?* Tu préfères un verre de vin? **c** *Do you smoke?* Tu fumes? **d** *Do you mind if I smoke?* Ça te dérange si je fume? **e** *Do you want a cigarette?* Tu veux une cigarette? **f** *Are you hungry?* As-tu faim? **g** *Would you like to go to a restaurant?* Tu veux aller au restaurant? **h** *Are you tired?* Tu es fatigué(e)? **i** *Do you like going to the cinema?* Tu aimes aller au cinéma? **j** *Have you got someone special?* Tu as quelqu'un dans ta vie?

1.8

I **a** Appuyez sur le bouton. *Press the button.* **b** Composez votre code. *Enter your PIN.* **c** Parlez dans le micro. *Speak into the microphone.* **d** Attendez le bip sonore. *Wait for the tone.* **e** Poussez. *Push.* **f** Tirez. *Pull.* **g** Compostez votre billet. *Cancel your (bus/train) ticket.* **h** Signez ici. *Sign here.* **i** Ne quittez pas. *Please hold the line.* **j** Patientez. *Wait*

III **a** Avez **b** Allez **c** Buvez **d** Mangez **e** Bougez **f** Fumez **g** Faites **h** Allez **i** Couchez-vous **j** Dormez

V **a** *Don't smoke*. Ne fumez pas. **b** *Dont' walk on the grass*. Ne marchez pas sur l'herbe. **c** *Don't eat in the shop*. Ne mangez pas dans le magasin. **d** *Don't leave your luggage here*. Ne laissez pas vos bagages ici. **e** *Don't cross the road*. Ne traversez pas la rue. **f** *Don't lean out of the window*. Ne vous penchez pas au-dehors. **g** *Don't drink the water*. Ne buvez pas cette eau. **h** *Don't wait here*. N'attendez pas ici. **i** *Don't put ski boots on the counter*. Ne mettez pas vos chaussures de ski sur le comptoir. **j** *Don't wear black*. Ne portez pas de noir. **k** *Don't open the door*. N'ouvrez pas la porte.

VI **a** *Can you manage*? Vous vous débrouillez? **b** *Are you interested in the firm*? Vous vous intéressez à l'entreprise? **c** *Are you responsible for buying*? Vous vous occupez des achats?

VII **a** Entrez **b** Mettez-vous **c** Trouvez **d** Courez **e** Ecartez **f** Tendez **g** Rentrez **h** Baissez **i** Pliez **j** Mettez **k** Bougez

VIII **a** Sortez **b** Tournez **c** Prenez **d** Continuez **e** Traversez **f** Suivez **g** Tournez

1.9

I **a** joue **b** chante **c** surfe **d** aime **e** loue **f** vend **g** achète **h** prête **i** prépare **j** signe

II **a** est **b** habite **c** va **d** prend **e** passe **f** arrive **g** a **h** laisse **i** fait **j** retourne

III **a** se réveille **b** se lève **c** se lave **d** se douche **e** se brosse **f** se rase **g** s'habille **h** se chausse **i** prend **j** sort

1.10

I **a** doivent **b** ont **c** vont **d** garent **e** font **f** sortent **g** trouvent **h** cherchent **i** trouvent **j** appellent

II **a** ne parlent pas **b** ne mangent pas **c** ne portent pas **d** ne boivent pas **e** ne passent pas **f** n'ont pas **g** ne vont pas **h** ne lisent pas **i** ne regardent pas **j** n'habitent pas

III **a** Partent-ils . . . ? **b** Prennent-ils . . . ? **c** Vont-ils . . . ? **d** Ont-ils . . . ? **e** Louent-ils . . . ? **f** Jouent-ils . . . ? **g** Font-ils . . . ? **h** Ont-ils . . . ?

IV **a** vont-ils? **b** partent-ils? **c** voyagent-ils . . . ? **d** sont-ils . . . ? **e** font-ils? **f** invitent-ils? **g** restent-ils . . . ?

V **a** ils/elles se couchent **b** ils/elles se douchent **c** ils/elles s'étonnent **d** ils/elles s'habillent **e** ils/elles s'intéressent à **f** ils/elles se lavent **g** ils/elles se lèvent **h** ils/elles se réveillent

VI **a** se reposent **b** se réveillent **c** se lèvent **d** se douchent **e** se préparent **f** sortent **g** vont **h** arrivent **i** s'ennuient **j** s'en vont

1.11

I **a** ai **b** suis **c** pars **d** prends **e** arrive **f** sors **g** attends **h** aime **i** m'ennuie **j** rentre

II **a** Nous avons un rendez-vous en ville. **b** Nous sommes prêt(e)s. **c** Nous partons de l'appartement. **d** Nous prenons le métro. **e** Nous arrivons à l'Opéra. **f** Nous sortons du métro sur la place de l'Opéra. **g** Nous attendons Pierre et Bénédicte. **h** Nous n'aimons pas attendre. **i** Nous nous ennuyons. **j** Nous rentrons chez nous.

III **a** Avez-vous un rendez-vous en ville? **b** Êtes-vous prêt(e)s? **c** Partez-vous de l'appartement? **d** Prenez-vous le métro? **e** Arrivez-vous à l'Opéra? **f** Sortez-vous du métro sur la place de l'Opéra? **g** Attendez-vous Pierre et Bénédicte? **h** N'aimez-vous pas attendre? **i** Vous ennuyez-vous? **j** Rentrez-vous chez vous?

IV **a** Il/Elle a un rendez-vous en ville. **b** Il/Elle est prêt(e). **c** Il/Elle sort de l'appartement. **d** Il/Elle prend le métro. **e** Il/Elle arrive à l'Opéra. **f** Il/Elle sort du métro sur la place de l'Opéra. **g** Il/Elle attend Pierre et Bénédicte. **h** Il/Elle n'aime pas attendre. **i** Il/Elle s'ennuie. **j** Il rentre chez lui./Elle rentre chez elle.

V **a** Ils/Elles ont un rendez-vous en ville **b** Ils/Elles sont prêt(e)s. **c** Ils/Elles sortent de l'appartement. **d** Ils/Elles prennent le métro. **e** Ils/Elles arrivent à l'Opéra. **f** Ils/Elles sortent du métro sur la place de l'Opéra. **g** Ils/Elles attendent Pierre et Bénédicte. **h** Ils/Elles n'aiment pas attendre. **i** Ils/Elles ennuient. **j** Ils/Elles rentrent chez eux.

1.13

I **a** avons **b** ai **c** a **d** As **e** ont **f** a **g** ont **h** Avez **i** a **j** ont

II **a** suis **b** est **c** sont **d** est **e** Es **f** est **g** est **h** est **i** Êtes **j** sommes

III **a** joué **b** mangé **c** fini **d** vendu **e** écouté **f** perdu **g** choisi **h** attendu **i** organisé **j** invité **k** lavé **l** demandé **m** fermé **n** poussé **o** tiré **p** oublié **q** sorti **r** entré **s** entendu **t** parti

IV **a** joué **b** dîné **c** téléphoné **d** discuté **e** assuré **f** décidé **g** envoyé **h** changé **i** imprimé **j** regardé

V **a** vu **b** fait **c** écrit **d** mis **e** imprimé **f** vu **g** dû **h** été

VI **a** a gagné **b** a voulu **c** a lu **d** a acheté **e** a décidé **f** a mis **g** a pris **h** a vu **i** a cru **j** a suivi **k** a fait **l** ont arrêté **m** a dû

VII **a** Stéphanie a lu son dernier roman. **b** Avez-vous lu le livre?/As-tu lu le livre? **c** Nous n'avons pas lu le livre. **d** Ils ont vu le film. **e** Stéphanie a vu le film hier. **f** Nous n'avons pas vu le film. **g** Avez-vous vu le film?/As-tu vu le film? **h** Stéphanie a écrit une lettre. **i** Je n'ai pas reçu de lettre. **j** Elle l'a mise à la poste hier. **k** Son mari a pris son parapluie. **l** Il a oublié son journal. **m** Ils n'ont pas compris. **n** Nous avons compris. **o** J'ai compris.

VIII **a** j'ai **b** tu as/vous avez **c** nous avons **d** ils/elles ont **e** il a **f** elle a **g** vous avez/tu as **h** John a **i** Avez-vous?/As-tu? **j** ma femme et moi avons

IX **a** sommes **b** suis **c** Êtes **d** sont **e** est **f** es **g** est **h** sont **i** êtes **j** sommes

X **a** allé **b** sorti **c** parti **d** arrivé **e** descendu **f** entré **g** monté **h** tombé **i** resté

XI **a** est **b** est **c** suis **d** est **e** sommes **f** sommes **g** est **h** est **i** suis

XII **a** née **b** mort **c** allée **d** partie **e** arrivée **f** allés **g** arrivé **h** venue **i** montée **j** tombée

XIII **a** allé **b** allée **c** allés **d** allé(e)s **e** allé(e)s **f** allé(e)s **g** allés **h** allé **i** allé(e) **j** allé(e)

XIV **a** me suis levé(e) **b** s'est levé **c** s'est levée **d** s'est levé **e** se sont levés **f** t'es levée **g** nous sommes levé(e)s **h** se sont levés **i** se sont levées **j** vous êtes levé(e)s

XV **a** nous sommes réveillé(e)s **b** nous sommes levé(e)s **c** nous sommes prommené(e)s **d** nous sommes trompé(e)s **e** nous sommes égaré(e)s

f nous sommes arrêté(e)s **g** nous sommes reposé(e)s **h** s'est énervée **i** s'est souvenue **j** me suis débrouillée

1.14

I a dormait **b** regardait **c** lisait **d** discutais **e** parlions **f** prenait **g** téléphonait **h** réparaient **i** jouaient

II a avait **b** avaient **c** avions **d** aviez **e** avais

III a était **b** étaient **c** étiez **d** était **e** étions

IV a attendais **b** écoutais **c** allions **d** lisait **e** attendait **f** sortait **g** étaient **h** faisait **i** regardiez **j** buvait

V a faisait **b** neigeait **e** avait **d** soufflait **e** brillait **f** pleuvait **g** se dissipait **h** faisait **i** avait **j** était

VI a habitaient; est née **b** était; a déménagé **c** avait; est né **d** a eu; avait **e** traversait; a grillé **f** a vu; attendait **g** avait; a passé **h** faisait; a décidé **i** suivait; a vu **j** travaillait; a recontré **k** était; a posé **l** faisait; se sont mariés

VII a Quand j'étais petit(e) . . . **b** Quand j'attendais le bus . . . **c** Il pleuvait. **d** Il faisait froid. **e** Il y avait du soleil.

1.15

I a vais **b** vas **c** va **d** allons **e** allez **f** vont **g** allez **h** vont **i** vais

II a vont **b** va **c** va **d** vont **e** va **f** va **g** va **h** allons **i** va **j** allez

III a regarderons **b** prépareras **c** mettrez **d** mangeront **e** prendra **f** sortirez **g** arriveront **h** entrerons **i** partirai **j** portera

IV a porterai **b** portera **c** portera **d** portera **e** porteront **f** porteront **g** porterons **h** porterez

V a irai **b** viendrez **c** feras **d** aurons **e** sera **f** verra **g** voudront **h** devrons **i** saurez **j** tiendront **k** faudra **l** pourrez

VI a partirons **b** arrivera **c** prendrons **d** aura **e** fera **f** déjeunerons **g** sortira **h** fera **i** devrons

1.16

I a je mangerais **b** je boirais **c** je dormirais **d** je parlerais **e** j'habiterais **f** j'achèterais **g** je demanderais **h** j'écouterais **i** je regarderais

II a jouerais **b** jouerait **c** joueraient **d** jouerions **e** joueriez

III a préférerais **b** préférerait **c** préféreraient **d** préférerions **e** préféreriez

IV a aimerais **b** aimerait **c** aimerait **d** aimeraient **e** aimeriez

V a voudrais **b** irais **c** aurais **d** verrais **e** irais **f** pourrais **g** serais **h** saurais **i** devrais **j** tiendrais

VI **a** pourrait **b** pourrions **c** pourrions **d** pourrais **e** pourriez **f** pourrait **g** pourraient **h** pourrions **i** pourrions **j** pourrions

1.17

I **a** venir **b** prendre **c** faire **d** être **e** avoir **f** avoir

1.19

I **a** Tournez/Tourne **b** Montez/Monte **c** Prenez/Prends **d** Continuez/Continue **e** Allez/Va **f** Regardez/Regarde **g** Traversez/Traverse **h** Prenez/Prends **i** Descendez/Descends

II **a** Préchauffez **b** Émincez **c** Battez **d** Mettez **e** Ajoutez **f** Mélangez **g** Beurrez **h** Versez **i** Mettez **j** Faites cuire

III **a** Regardez **b** Mangez **c** Buvez **d** Faites **e** Fermez **f** Ouvrez **g** Présentez **h** Parlez **i** Venez

1.20

I **a** Je ne suis jamais allé(e) en France. **b** Il n'a jamais vu Frédéric. **c** Nous n'avons jamais dîné au restaurant. **d** Ils n'ont jamais mangé de viande. **e** Vous n'avez jamais appris à nager? **f** Je ne vois plus Aline. **g** Elle ne fait plus de vélo. **h** Ils n'habitent plus Paris. **i** Il n'écoute plus sa femme. **j** Ils n'ont plus d'argent. **k** Je ne vois personne. **l** Je n'ai vu personne. **m** Jean-Luc n'a vu personne. **n** Personne n'a vu Jean-Luc. **o** Ils n'ont fait de mal à personne. **p** Il ne me reste que dix Euros. **q** Ils n'ont qu'une petite maison. **r** Il n'y a qu'une chambre. **s** M. Bériot n'a qu'un fils. **t** Nous n'avons qu'une imprimante noir et blanc. **u** Je n'ai rien. **v** Ils n'ont rien vu. **w** Nous n'avons rien entendu. **x** Vous ne faites rien! **y** Ils n'ont jamais rien fait!

II **a** Nous n'avons rien à manger. **b** Personne n'a fait les courses. **c** Je n'avais pas le temps d'aller en ville. **d** Il n'y a que du pain et du fromage. **e** Vous n'allez jamais au supermarché. **f** Je n'ai plus d'argent.

1.21

I **a** Quel **b** Quels **c** Quelles **d** Quelle

1.22

I **a** J'habite ici depuis . . . ans. **b** J'apprends le français depuis . . . ans. **c** Je connais mon meilleur ami/ma meilleure amie depuis . . . ans.

1.24

I **a** Nous avons raison. **b** Vous avez tort./Tu as tort. **c** J'ai chaud. **d** Il a soif. **e** Ils/Elles ont faim. **f** Nous avons froid. **g** J'ai soif. **h** J'ai besoin d'une bière. **i** Nous avons besoin d'une nouvelle voiture. **j** J'ai raison. **k** Ils/Elles ont tort. **k** J'ai très froid. **m** Ils/Elles ont chaud. **n** Nous avons soif. **o** J'ai peur des araignées. **p** Avez-vous soif?/As-tu soif? **q** Avez-vous froid?/As-tu froid? **r** Avez-vous chaud?/As-tu chaud? **s** Avez-vous faim?/As-tu faim? **t** Avez-vous raison?/As tu raison? **u** Vous avez tort!/Tu as tort! **v** Avez-vous peur?/As-tu peur? **w** Je n'ai pas peur. **x** Il n'a pas peur. **y** Nous n'avons pas peur. **z** Il a raison.

II **a** J'ai mal à la tête. **b** Avez-vous mal aux dents?/As-tu mal aux dents? **c** Elle a mal au pied. **d** J'ai mal aux bras. **e** Il a mal au genou. **f** Avez-vous mal à la tête?/As-tu mal à la tête? **g** Elle a mal aux oreilles. **h** Avez-vous mal au cœur?/As-tu mal au cœur? **i** Avez-vous mal au dos?/As-tu mal au dos? **j** Il a mal au dos.

2.2

I **a** la voiture **b** la valise **c** le sac **d** le portable **e** la calculette **f** le fichier **g** la carte bancaire **h** la réservation **i** le manteau **j** le billet **k** le ticket

II **a** la maison **b** la station-service **c** la gare **d** la rue **e** le boulevard **f** la station de métro **g** le magasin **h** la banque **i** la poste **j** le pont

III **a** l'appartement **b** le château **c** l'école **d** l'hôpital **e** l'église **f** la mairie **g** l'immeuble **h** l'hôtel **i** l'avenue **j** l'entrée **k** l'arbre **l** le bébé **m** l'eau **n** l'enfant **o** l'homme **p** l'horloge **q** la rivière **r** la rue **s** la ville **t** le village

IV **a** le dimanche **b** la salade **c** le Canada **d** la Loire **e** le gâteau **f** le printemps **g** le litre **h** le basket-ball **i** le tennis **j** le ski **k** la boucherie **l** le lundi **m** la pâtisserie **n** la France **o** le hockey **p** le marché **q** la Dordogne **r** le sweat-shirt **s** le château **t** le français

V **a** les animaux **b** les oiseaux **c** les genoux **d** les chevaux **e** les bateaux **f** les journaux **g** les châteaux **h** les neveux **i** les cadeaux

VI **a** les fils **b** les Français **c** les Anglais **d** les croix **e** les repas **f** les feux **g** les pneus **h** les choux **i** les bois **j** les souris

2.3

I **a** un frère **b** une sœur **c** un grand-père **d** une grand-mère **e** un oncle **f** une tante **g** un beau-père **h** une cousine **i** une belle-mère **j** un chien

2.4

I **a** du **b** de l' **c** du **d** du **e** des **f** du **g** du **h** des **i** de la **j** du

II **a** de la **b** du **c** de la **d** du **e** du **f** du **g** du **h** du **i** de l' **j** du

III **a** un **b** un **c** des **d** une **e** une **f** un **g** des **h** des **i** un **j** un

IV **a** Il n'y a pas de ketchup. **b** Il n'y a pas de confiture. **c** Il n'y a pas de mayonnaise. **d** Il n'y a pas de sucre. **e** Il n'y a pas de lait. **f** Il n'y a pas de beurre. **g** Il n'y a pas de fromage. **h** Il n'y a pas de soupe. **i** Il n'y a pas de jus d'orange. **j** Il n'y a pas de yaourt.

V **a** Je ne mange pas de noix. **b** Je ne mange pas de cacahuètes. **c** Je ne mange pas de sucreries. **d** Je ne mange pas de viande. **e** Je ne mange pas de poisson. **f** Je ne mange pas de laitue. **g** Je ne mange pas de tomates.

h Je ne mange pas de légumes. **i** Je ne mange pas de pain. **j** Je ne mange pas d'escargots.

VI **a** J'ai beaucoup de livres. **b** J'ai beaucoup de BDs. **c** J'ai beaucoup de CDs. **d** J'ai beaucoup de photos.

VII **a** J'ai assez d'essence. **b** J'ai assez d'argent. **c** J'ai assez d'informations. **d** J'ai assez de temps. **e** J'ai assez de catalogues.

VIII **a** J'ai trop de travail. **b** J'ai trop d'invitations. **c** J'ai trop de déplacements. **d** J'ai trop de bagages. **e** J'ai trop de papiers.

2.5

I **a** à la vanille **b** au citron **c** à la pistache **d** au cassis **e** à l'abricot **f** au chocolat **g** à la banane **h** à la fraise **i** à l'orange **j** à la mangue

II **a** au jambon **b** au poulet **c** au saucisson **d** au fromage **e** à la sardine **f** au thon **g** aux rillettes **h** au camembert

III **a** à la plage **b** à l'hôtel **c** à la piscine **d** à l'hôpital **e** au musée **f** au cinéma **g** au théâtre **h** à la station-service **i** à la banque **j** à la gare

IV **a** à l'église St-Ouen **b** à la cathédrale Jeanne d'Arc **c** au Gros Horloge **d** à l'Hôtel de Ville **e** à la rue des Capucines **f** au musée du Théâtre **g** à l'office de tourisme **h** à la Seine **i** à la Place du marché **j** aux toilettes publiques

3.1

I **a** Il **b** Ils **c** J' **d** vous **e** Nous **f** Elles **g** Elle **h** Ils **i** tu **j** Il

3.2

I **a** me **b** him **c** us **d** them **e** you **f** them **g** it **h** them **i** us **j** you

II **a** me **b** le **c** les **d** la **e** les **f** le **g** le **h** les **i** les **j** vous/t' **k** nous **l** les **m** l' **n** vous **o** m' **p** l' **q** les **r** l' **s** l' **t** le

III **a** Il l'a vu. **b** Il les a vus. **c** Il les a vues. **d** Il l'a perdue. **e** Il l'a achetée. **f** Il l'a trouvée. **g** Il l'a donnée . . .

IV **a** aimée **b** lus **c** regardées **d** conduite **e** signés **f** dits **g** trahi

3.3

I **a** me **b** them **c** them **d** me **e** him **f** me **g** them **h** her **i** them **j** him

II **a** lui **b** leur **c** me **d** leur **e** nous **f** vous/te **g** lui **h** nous **i** lui **j** leur

3.4

I **a** Monique y habite. **b** J'y vais. **c** Nous y allons au moins trois fois par mois. **d** Y êtes-vous jamais allés? **e** Ils y mangent souvent. **f** Il y faisait beau. **g** Nous y avons fait de la planche à voile. **h** Il y a écouté le Requiem de Mozart. **i** Nous y achetons nos fruits et nos légumes. **j** Y manges-tu souvent?

3.5

I **a** J'en ai beaucoup. **b** Il n'en a pas. **c** Il en a trois. **d** Combien en avez-vous? **e** Nous en avons beaucoup de différents. **f** En avez-vous? **g** Ils en ont trois. **h** En-avez vous une? **i** Oui, j'en ai une. **j** Mon ami n'en a pas.

II **a** y aller **b** le payer **c** l'utiliser **d** en acheter (une) **e** y aller **f** le lire

3.6

I **a** Il m'a vu(e). **b** Elle l'a vu. **c** Il l'a achetée. **d** Elle ne l'a pas aimé. **e** Je peux le faire. **f** Je ne peux pas le faire. **g** Nous sommes y allé(e)s. **h** Ils/Elles nous ont accompagné(e)s. **i** J'en ai acheté. **j** Je les ai jetés.

II **a** Il me l'a donné. **b** Je le lui ai donné. **c** Elle le leur a donné. **d** Ils vous l'ont donné. **e** Vous nous l'avez donné. **f** Elle le lui a acheté. **g** Il l'a lu. **h** Il nous l'a donné. **i** Nous vous l'avons donné. **j** Ils le leur ont lu.

3.7

I **a** lui **b** elle **c** elles **d** elle **e** lui, lui **f** toi **g** nous **h** eux **i** vous **j** lui

II **a** moi **b** lui **c** nous **d** elle **e** vous/toi **f** lui **g** moi **h** lui **i** elle **j** nous

3.9

I **a** Que porte Jean-Luc?/Qu'est-ce que Jean-Luc porte? **b** Qui/Qui est-ce qui joue au foot? **c** Que mangeons-nous?/Qu'est-ce que nous mangeons? **d** Que fait Jérôme?/Qu'est-ce que Jérôme fait? **e** Que veux-je?/Qu'est-ce que je veux? **f** Que buvez-vous?/Qu'est-ce que vous buvez? **g** Qui/Qui est-ce qui va au cinéma?

3.10

I **a** le mien **b** les miens **c** la sienne **d** les siens **e** la vôtre **f** les leurs **g** la vôtre **h** les nôtres **i** les vôtres

3.11

I **a** qui **b** que **c** dont **d** que **e** dont **f** qui

3.13

I **a** ceux-ci **b** celle-ci **c** celui-là **d** celles-là **e** celles-ci **f** celui-là **g** celui-ci **h** ceux-là

4.1

I **a** *tall, sporty* **b** *short, dark, blue-grey* **c** *new, blue* **d** *smart, casual* **e** *small, big* **f** *small, bubbly* **g** *large* **h** *older, younger* **i** *favourite* **j** *hot, black*

II

	Singular		Plural	
	masculine	**feminine**	**masculine**	**feminine**
a	content	contente	contents	contentes
b	triste	triste	tristes	tristes
c	court	courte	courts	courtes
d	grand	grande	grands	grandes
e	faible	faible	faibles	faibles
f	fort	forte	forts	fortes
g	intelligent	intelligente	intelligents	intelligentes
h	stupide	stupide	stupides	stupides
i	joli	jolie	jolis	jolies
j	laid	laide	laids	laides
k	marrant	marrante	marrants	marrantes
l	méchant	méchante	méchants	méchantes
m	mauvais	mauvaise	mauvais	mauvaises
n	jeune	jeune	jeunes	jeunes
o	large	large	larges	larges
p	mince	mince	minces	minces
q	moderne	moderne	modernes	modernes
r	propre	propre	propres	propres
s	sale	sale	sales	sales
t	aimable	aimable	aimables	aimables

III **a** courts **b** content **c** petite **d** grands **e** jolie **f** minces **g** noirs **h** intelligente **i** méchante **j** marrants **k** petite **l** calme **m** moderne **n** grandes **o** petit **p** grand **q** petite **r** grandes **s** jolie **t** modernes

IV **a** actif **b** sportive **c** sportives **d** paresseux **e** vieille **f** ambitieux **g** heureuses **h** ennuyeux **i** heureux **j** paresseux **k** sérieuse **l** douce **m** ambitieux **n** affreuse **o** vieux **p** fausse **q** généreuse **r** ennuyeuses **s** affreuses **t** Joyeux

V **a** gros **b** grosse **c** gentille **d** gentils **e** belle **f** beau **g** bonnes **h** bons **i** naturelle **j** naturelles **k** ancienne **l** ancien **m** Bas **n** basse **o** nouveau **p** nouvel **q** nouvelles **r** belle **s** nouvelle **t** bonnes

VI **a** premier **b** première **c** dernière **d** dernier **e** secs **f** sèches **g** blanc **h** blanches **i** blanche **j** chers **k** chère **l** fier **m** fiers **n** dernière **o** dernier **p** grec **q** grecques **r** public **s** publique **t** sec **u** première **v** blancs

4.2

I **a** rouge **b** vertes **c** grise **d** bleue **e** bleue **f** rouges **g** jaune **h** rouges **i** bleu **j** jaunes

II **a** bleu-vert **b** marron **c** bleu marine **d** ivoire **e** parme **f** bleu clair **g** blanches **h** rose pâle **i** rose foncé **j** turquoise

4.3

I **a** une jeune enterprise **b** une jacinthe bleue **c** un enfant sage **d** un petit bijou **e** une belle femme **f** un après-midi paresseux **g** un vieux château **h** une bonne idée **i** un petit chat noir **j** un gros rat **k** une histoire intéressante **l** une jolie couleur **m** une grosse erreur **n** un philosophe moderne **o** un film ennuyeux **p** un long voyage **q** une mauvaise expérience **r** une grand ville **s** des falaises blanches **t** un penseur nouveau

4.4

I **a** M. Gilbert l'a vu de ses propres yeux. **b** Je vais vous présenter, chers auditeurs, un auteur contemporain. **c** Jérôme est un ancien élève de mon lycée. **d** Je n'ai plus de chaussettes propres. **e** La voiture la plus chère est une Ferrari. **f** Mon oncle nous a montré la ville ancienne. **g** Des millions de pauvres cailles sont tuées chaque année pendant la saison de la chasse. **h** Les familles pauvres habitent dans des bidonvilles. **i** La seule solution, c'est d'aller voir par vous-même. **j** L'homme seul qui attend le bus, c'est M. Robert.

4.5

I **a** plus timide **b** plus grande **c** plus difficile **d** plus intéressante **e** plus haut **f** plus long

II **a** moins chère **b** moins grande **c** moins bonne **d** moins intéressante

III **a** moins grand que **b** plus grand que **c** aussi grand que **d** moins grand que **e** moins grand que **f** plus grande que

IV **a** plus haut que **b** moins longue que **c** plus chaud qu' **d** aussi belle que **e** plus fatigant que

V **a** meilleur **b** meilleures **c** meilleure **d** meilleurs **e** meilleur **f** meilleurs **g** meilleures **h** meilleures

4.6

I **a** la plus haute **b** le plus long **c** la plus profonde **d** le plus grand **e** le plus long **f** le plus long **g** le plus grand **h** le plus connu **i** le plus vieux **j** la plus forte

II **a** meilleur **b** meilleure **c** meilleure **d** meilleure **e** meilleur

4.7

I **a** mon **b** mes **c** mon **d** mon **e** mon **f** mon **g** mon **h** ma **i** mon **j** mon

II **a** mon **b** ma **c** mon **d** mes **e** mes **f** mon **g** mon **h** mon **i** mes **j** mon

III **a** Ce sont mes enfants. **b** C'est mon mari. **c** C'est ma femme. **d** C'est mon père. **e** C'est ma mère. **f** C'est ma sœur. **g** Ce sont mes frères. **h** Ce sont mes grands-parents. **i** C'est mon cousin. **j** C'est mon fils. **k** C'est ma fille.

IV **a** Ce sont tes enfants. **b** C'est ton père. **c** C'est ta mère. **d** Ce sont tes sœurs. **e** C'est ton frère. **f** Ce sont tes grands-parents. **g** C'est ta fille. **h** C'est ton fils. **i** Ce sont tes chiens. **j** C'est ton chat.

V **a** Comment s'appellent tes collègues? **b** Comment s'appelle ton/ta collègue? **c** Comment s'appelle ton copain? **d** Comment s'appellent tes copines? **e** Comment s'appellent tes amis? **f** Comment s'apellent tes amies? **g** Comment s'appelle ton ami? **h** Comment s'appelle ton amie? **i** Comment s'appelle ta petite amie? **j** Comment s'appelle ton petit ami?

VI **a** Son **b** Son **c** Son **d** Sa **e** Son **f** Sa **g** Son **h** Son **i** Son **j** Sa

VII **a** Son **b** Son **c** Son **d** Sa **e** ses **f** Son **g** Sa **h** Sa **i** Son **j** Sa

VIII **a** C'est notre maison. **b** C'est notre appartement. **c** C'est notre balcon. **d** C'est notre cave. **e** Ce sont nos vins. **f** C'est notre garage. **g** C'est notre voiture. **h** C'est notre jardin. **i** Ce sont nos arbres. **j** C'est notre pelouse.

IX **a** C'est votre bureau? **b** C'est votre chaise? **c** C'est votre ordinateur? **d** Ce sont vos papiers? **e** C'est votre manteau? **f** Ce sont vos gants? **g** C'est votre parapluie? **h** Ce sont vos affaires? **i** C'est votre portefeuille? **j** Ce sont vos clés?

X **a** C'est leur voiture. **b** C'est leur garage. **c** Ce sont leurs vélos. **d** C'est leur jardin. **e** Ce sont leurs fleurs. **f** Ce sont leurs plantes. **g** C'est leur maison. **h** C'est leur porte. **i** Ce sont leurs fenêtres. **j** C'est leur balcon.

4.8

I **a** cet **b** cette **c** ce **d** Ces **e** Ces **f** Cet **g** Cette **h** Ces **i** Cet **j** ce

4.9

I **a** quel **b** quelle **c** quelle **d** quelles **e** quel **f** quel **g** quel **h** Quelles

5.2

I **a** lentement **b** Il a refusé net. **c** Ce n'est pas vrai! **d** C'est trop cher. **e** Parlez plus fort, s'il vous plaît.

6.2

a Je vais à la plage. **b** Je vais au bureau. **c** Je vais à l'hôtel. **d** Je vais au marché. **e** Je vais au musée. **f** Je vais à la banque. **g** Je vais à l'aéroport. **i** Je vais au distributeur. **j** Je vais à la gare.

II **a** à **b** à **c** aux **d** au **e** au **f** au **g** au **h** aux **i** au **j** au

III **a** Je vais au Havre. **b** Je vais au Mans. **c** Je vais aux Champs-Elysées. **d** Je vais aux Deux-Alpes. **e** Je vais au Lavandou. **f** Je vais au Louvre. **g** Je vais aux Menuires. **h** Je vais à la Cité des Sciences et de l'Industrie.

IV **a** Je voudrais un sandwich au jambon. **b** Je voudrais un sandwich au fromage. **c** Je voudrais un sandwich à la banane. **d** Je voudrais un sandwich à la confiture. **e** Je voudrais un sandwich aux tomates. **f** Je voudrais un sandwich au thon. **g** Je voudrais un sandwich au lard. **h** Je voudrais un sandwich au saucisson.

6.3

I **a** du Japon **b** du train **c** des monuments **d** du Louvre **e** de la Concorde **f** de Bir-Hakeim **g** de la Tour Eiffel **h** de la Place du Trocadéro

II **a** du jambon **b** des pommes de terre **c** des tomates **d** de la salade **e** de tomates **f** de la moutarde **g** de l'huile **h** du sel **i** du poivre

III **a** une bouteille de vin **b** un verre d'eau **c** une tasse de café **d** du sucre **e** une omelette au fromage **f** du pain **g** une glace à la fraise **h** une salade de fruits

6.4

I **a** 3 **b** 6 **c** 1 **d** 2 **e** 4 **f** 5

II **a** sur la table **b** sur l'étagère **c** sous le placard **d** dans le tiroir **e** derrière le rideau

6.7

I **a** Il prend les cours d'espagnol depuis deux ans. **b** Il habite à Paris depuis cinq ans. **c** M. Proudhon habite à Paris depuis deux mois. **d** Il joue de la guitare depuis un an. **e** Il travaille dans cette boulangerie depuis six mois. **f** Il joue aux échecs depuis son enfance. **g** Constance est végétarienne depuis l'âge de treize ans. **h** Elle fait du ski depuis cinq ans. **i** Ils font de la planche depuis l'été dernier. **j** Ils regardent des films de science fiction depuis trois ans. **k** Ils sortent ensemble depuis six mois.

Avoir and être

Infinitive	Present tense		Perfect Imperfect	Future Conditional Subjunctive
avoir *to have*	j'ai tu as il a	nous avons vous avez ils ont	j'ai eu j'avais	j'aurai j'aurais que j'aie
être *to be*	je suis tu es il est	nous sommes vous êtes ils sont	j'ai été j'étais	je serai je serais que je sois

Regular **-er**, **-ir** and **-re** verbs

Infinitive	Present tense		Perfect Imperfect	Future Conditional Subjunctive
parler *to speak*	je parle tu parles il parle	nous parlons vous parlez ils parlent	j'ai parlé je parlais	je parlerai je parlerais que je parle
finir *to finish*	je finis tu finis il finit	nous finissons vous finissez ils finissent	j'ai fini je finissais	je finirai je finirais que je finisse
répondre *to reply*	je réponds tu réponds il répond	nous répondons vous répondez ils répondent	j'ai répondu je répondais	je répondrai je répondrais que je réponde

Irregular verbs

Infinitive	Present tense		Perfect Imperfect	Future Conditional Subjunctive
acheter *to buy*	j'achète tu achètes il achète	nous achetons vous achetez ils achètent	j'ai acheté j'achetais	j'achèterai j'achèterais que j'achète
admettre *to admit*	*see:* mettre			
aller *to go*	je vais tu vas il va	nous allons vous allez ils vont	je suis allé(e) j'allais	j'irai j'irais que j'aille
apercevoir *to catch sight of*	j'aperçois tu aperçois il aperçoit	nous apercevons vous apercevez ils aperçoivent	j'ai aperçu j'apercevais	j'apercevrai j'apercevrais que j'aperçoive
apparaître *to appear*	*see:* paraître			
apprendre *to learn*	*see:* prendre			
s'asseoir *to sit down*	je m'assieds tu t'assieds il s'assied	nous nous asseyons vous vous asseyez ils s'asseyent	je me suis assis(e) je m'asseyais	je m'assiérai je m'assiérais que je m'asseye
atteindre *to reach*	j'atteins tu atteins il atteint	nous atteignons vous atteignez ils atteignent	j'ai atteint j'attegnais	j'atteindrai j'atteindrais que j'atteigne
battre *to beat*	je bats tu bats il bat	nous battons vous battez ils battent	j'ai battu je battais	je battrai je battrais que je batte
boire *to drink*	je bois tu bois il boit	nous buvons vous buvez ils boivent	j'ai bu je buvais	je boirai je boirais que je boive
commencer *to begin*	je commence tu commences il commence	nous commençons vous commencez ils commencent	j'ai commencé je commençais	je commencerai je commencerais que je commence
comprendre *to understand*	*see:* prendre			

Infinitive	Present tense		Perfect Imperfect	Future Conditional Subjunctive
conduire *to drive*	je conduis tu conduis il conduit	nous conduisons vous conduisez ils conduisent	j'ai conduit je conduisais	je conduirai je conduirais que je conduise
connaître *to know*	je connais tu connais il connaît	nous connaissons vous connaissez ils connaissent	j'ai connu je connaissais	je connaîtrai je connaîtrais que je connaisse
coudre *to sew*	je couds tu couds il coud	nous cousons vous cousez ils cousent	j'ai cousu je cousais	je coudrai je coudrais que je couse
courir *to run*	je cours tu cours il court	nous courons vous courez ils courent	j'ai couru je courais	je courrai je courrais que je coure
couvrir *to cover*	*see:* ouvrir			
craindre *to fear*	je crains tu crains il craint	nous craignons vous craignez ils craignent	j'ai craint je craignais	je craindrai je craindrais que je craigne
croire *to believe*	je crois tu crois ils croit	nous croyons vous croyez ils croient	j'ai cru je croyais	je croirai je croirais que je croie
cueillir *to gather*	je cueille tu cueilles il cueille	nous cueillons vous cueillez ils cueillent	j'ai cueilli je cueillais	je cueillerai je cueillerais que je cueille
découvrir *to discover*	*see:* ouvrir			
décrire *to describe*	*see:* écrire			
devoir *to have to*	je dois tu dois il doit	nous devons vous devez ils doivent	j'ai dû je devais	je devrai je devrais que je doive
dire *to say*	je dis tu dis il dit	nous disons vous dites ils disent	j'ai dit je disais	je dirai je dirais que je dise
dormir *to sleep*	je dors tu dors il dort	nous dormons vous dormez ils dorment	j'ai dormi je dormais	je dormirai je dormirais que je dorme

Infinitive	Present tense		Perfect Imperfect	Future Conditional Subjunctive
écrire *to write*	j'écris tu écris il écrit	nous écrivons vous écrivez ils écrivent	j'ai écrit j'écrivais	j'écrirai j'écrirais que j'écrive
envoyer *to send*	j'envoie tu envoies il envoie	nous envoyons vous envoyez ils envoient	j'ai envoyé j'envoyais	j'enverrai j'enverrais que j'envoie
essayer *to try*	j'essaie tu essaies il essaie	nous essayons vous essayez ils essaient	j'ai essayé j'essayais	j'essayerai j'essayerais que j'essaie
faire *to do/make*	je fais tu fais il fait	nous faisons vous faites ils font	j'ai fait je faisais	je ferai je ferais que je fasse
falloir *to be necessary*	il faut		il a fallu il fallait	il faudra il faudrait qu'il faille
introduire *to introduce*	*see:* conduire			
lever *to raise/lift*	je lève tu lèves il lève	nous levons vous levez ils lèvent	j'ai levé je levais	je lèverai je lèverais que je lève
lire *to read*	je lis tu lis il lit	nous lisons vous lisez ils lisent	j'ai lu je lisais	je lirai je lirais que je lise
manger *to eat*	je mange tu manges il mange	nous mangeons vous mangez ils mangent	j'ai mangé je mangeais	je mangerai je mangerais que je mange
mettre *to put*	je mets tu mets il met	nous mettons vous mettez ils mettent	j'ai mis je mettais	je mettrai je mettrais que je mette
mourir *to die*	je meurs tu meurs il meurt	nous mourons vous mourez ils meurent	je suis mort(e) je mourais	je mourrai je mourrais que je meure
nager *to swim*	*see:* manger			
naître *to be born*	je nais tu nais il naît	nous naissons vous naissez ils naissent	je suis né(e) je naissais	je naîtrai je naîtrais que je naisse

Infinitive	Present tense		Perfect Imperfect	Future Conditional Subjunctive
offrir *to offer*	j'offre tu offres il offre	nous offrons vous offrez ils offrent	j'ai offert j'offrais	j'offrirai j'offrirais que j'offre
ouvrir *to open*	j'ouvre tu ouvres il ouvre	nous ouvrons vous ouvrez ils ouvrent	j'ai ouvert j'ouvrais	j'ouvrirai j'ouvrirais que j'ouvre
paraître *to appear/ seem*	je parais tu parais il paraît	nous paraissons vous paraissez ils paraissent	j'ai paru je paraissais	je paraîtrai je paraîtrais que je paraisse
partir *to leave*	je pars tu pars ils part	nous partons vous partez ils partent	je suis parti(e) je partais	je partirai je partirais que je parte
payer *to pay*	je paie tu paies il paie	nous payons vous payez ils paient	j'ai payé je payais	je paierai je paierais que je paie
permettre *to permit*	*see:* mettre			
plaindre *to pity*	je plains tu plains il plaint	nous plaignons vous plaignez ils plaignent	j'ai plaint je plaignais	je plaindrai je plaindrais que je plaigne
pleuvoir *to rain*	il pleut		il a plu il pleuvait	il pleuvra il pleuvrait qu'il pleuve
poursuivre *to pursue*	*see:* suivre			
pouvoir *to be able to*	je peux tu peux il peut	nous pouvons vous pouvez ils peuvent	j'ai pu je pouvais	je pourrai je pourrais que je puisse
prendre *to take*	je prends tu prends il prend	nous prenons vous prenez ils prennent	j'ai pris je prenais	je prendrai je prendrais que je prenne
recevoir *to receive*	je reçois tu reçois il reçoit	nous recevons vous recevez ils reçoivent	j'ai reçu je recevais	je recevrai je recevrais que je reçoive
reconnaître *to recognise*	*see:* connaître			

Infinitive	Present tense		Perfect Imperfect	Future Conditional Subjunctive
résoudre *to resolve*	je résous tu résous il résout	nous résolvons vous résolvez ils résolvent	j'ai résolu je résolvais	je résoudrai je résoudrais que je résolve
rire *to laugh*	je ris tu ris il rit	nous rions vous riez ils rient	j'ai ri je riais	je rirai je rirais que je rie
rompre *to break* *(a contract, etc.)*	je romps tu romps il romp	nous rompons vous rompez ils rompent	j'ai rompu je rompais	je romprai je romprais que je rompe
savoir *to know*	je sais tu sais il sait	nous savons vous savez ils savent	j'ai su je savais	je saurai je saurais que je sache
sentir *to smell*	je sens tu sens il sent	nous sentons vous sentez ils sentent	j'ai senti je sentais	je sentirai je sentirais que je sente
servir *to serve*	je sers tu sers il sert	nous servons vous servez ils servent	j'ai servi je servais	je servirai je servirais que je serve
sortir *to go out*	je sors tu sors il sort	nous sortons vous sortez ils sortent	je suis sorti(e) je sortais	je sortirai je sortirais que je sorte
souffrir *to suffer*	je souffre tu souffres il souffre	nous souffrons vous souffrez ils souffrent	j'ai souffert je souffrais	je souffrirai je souffrirais que je souffre
sourire *to smile*	je souris tu souris il sourit	nous sourions vous souriez ils sourient	j'ai souri je souriais	je sourirai je sourirais que je sourie
suivre *to follow*	je suis tu suis il suit	nous suivons vous suivez ils suivent	j'ai suivi je suivais	je suivrai je suivrais que je suive
tenir *to hold*	je tiens tu tiens il tient	nous tenons vous tenez ils tiennent	j'ai tenu je tenais	je tiendrai je tiendrais que je tienne
vaincre *to defeat*	je vaincs tu vaincs il vainc	nous vainquons vous vainquez ils vainquent	j'ai vaincu je vainquais	je vaincrai je vaincrais que je vainque

Infinitive	Present tense		Perfect Imperfect	Future Conditional Subjunctive
valoir *to be worth*	je vaux tu vaux il vaut	nous valons vous valez ils valent	j'ai valu je valais	je vaudrai je vaudrais que je vale
venir *to come*	je viens tu viens il vient	nous venons vous venez ils viennent	je suis venu(e) je venais	je viendrai je viendrais que je vienne
vivre *to live*	je vis tu vis il vit	nous vivons vous vivez ils vivent	j'ai vécu je vivais	je vivrai je vivrais que je vive
voir *to see*	je vois tu vois il voit	nous voyons vous voyez ils voient	j'ai vu je voyais	je verrai je verrais que je voie
vouloir *to want*	je veux tu veux il veut	nous voulons vous voulez ils veulent	j'ai voulu je voulais	je voudrai je voudrais que je veuille

Verbs and prepositions

These verbs are followed by prepositions in English, but not in French.

attendre — *to wait for*
J'attends le bus. — *I'm waiting for the bus.*
chercher — *to look for*
Il cherche son parapluie. — *He's looking for his umbrella.*
demander — *to ask for*
Je demande une réponse. — *I'm asking for a reply.*
écouter — *to listen to*
Elle écoute un CD de Céline Dion. — *She's listening to a Céline Dion CD.*
habiter — *to live in/at*
Mon collègue habite Paris. — *My colleague lives in Paris.*
mettre — *to put (on)*
Marianne met son impérméable. — *Marianne puts on her raincoat.*
payer — *to pay for*
Je paie l'addition. — *I pay the bill.*
regarder — *to look at/watch*
Il regarde sa montre. — *He's looking at his watch.*
sortir — *to go out*
Elle sort. — *She's going out.*

Some verbs which don't require a preposition in English are followed by **de** in French. These are some of the most commonly used ones.

s'apercevoir de — *to notice*
Il s'est aperçu de l'heure. — *He noticed the time.*
changer de — *to change*
Elle a changé de robe. — *She changed her dress.*
discuter de — *to discuss*
Ils ont discuté des nouvelles. — *They discussed the news.*
douter de — *to doubt*
Elle doute de son intention. — She doubts his intention.
jouer de — *to play (an instrument)*
Elle joue du piano. — *She plays the piano.*
manquer de — *to lack*
Il manque d'humour. — *He lacks humour.*
se méfier de — *to mistrust*
Elle se méfie de son collègue. — *She mistrusts her colleague.*
se servir de — *to use*
Il se sert des idées de son ami. — *He uses his friend's ideas.*
se souvenir de — *to remember*
Je me souviens des vacances. — *I remember the holidays.*
se tromper de — *to mistake*
Il s'est trompé de route. — *He mistook the way/took a wrong turn.*

These are some of the verbs which are followed by **à** in French.

aider quelqu'un à — *to help someone*
J'ai aidé mon père à classer. — *I helped my father with the fitting.*
s'apprêter à — *to prepare to*
Il s'est apprêté à aller à la réunion. — *He prepared to go to the meeting.*
arriver à — *to manage to*
Elle est arrivée à ouvrir la boîte. — *She managed to open the tin.*
assister à — *to attend*
J'ai assisté à deux réunions. — *I attended two meetings.*
commencer à — *to begin to*
Elle a commencé à chanter. — *She began to sing.*
demander à — *to ask*
J'ai demandé à mon collègue de m'aider. — *I asked my colleague to help me.*
des(obéir) à — *to (dis)obey*
L'enfant a (dés)obéi à son père. — *The child (dis)obeyed its father.*
(dé)plaire à — *to (dis)please*
Elle fait tout pour plaire à ses enfants. — *She does everything to please her children.*
s'intéresser à — *to be interested in*
Je m'intéresse au cinéma comme métier. — *I'm interested in a career in the cinema.*
jouer à — *to play a sport*
Il joue au tennis. — *He plays tennis.*

penser à	*to think about*
Je pense à lui.	*I'm thinking about him.*
renoncer à	*to renounce/give up*
Il a renoncé à fumer.	*He gave up smoking.*
répondre à	*to reply to*
Il a répondu à mes questions.	*He replied to my questions.*
résister à	*to resist*
Il a résisté à ses cajoleries.	*He resisted her coaxing.*
ressembler à	*to resemble*
Il ressemble à son père.	*He resembles his father.*
réussir à	*to succeed in*
Il a réussi à envoyer le fax à temps.	*He succeeded in sending the fax in time.*
téléphoner à	*to ring (up)*
Il a téléphoné à son collègue.	*He rang his colleague.*
tenir à	*to be determined to*
Je tiens à y aller.	*I'm determined to go (there).*